HOW TO MAKE

SEWING PATTERNS

DONALD H. MᶜCUNN

PHOTOGRAPHS BY

ROBIN LEW

DESIGN ENTERPRISES OF SAN FRANCISCO

To Dr. Alfred Azevedo, who opened up the
doors of public education to my ideas.

To Dr. Paul D. Reinhardt, whose inspiration
is the cornerstone of this book.

And to my wife, whose continued support
has made all of my endeavors possible.

Photographic Model: Virginia S. Ashburn

Library of Congress Catalog Card Number: 77-85078
Revised Edition

ISBN: 0-932538-00-2

First Printing, November 1977
Second Printing, June 1978
Third Printing, January 1980
Fourth Printing, November, 1981
Fifth Printing, March 1982
Sixth Printing, September 1984
Seventh Printing, December 1985
Eighth Printing, June 1992
Ninth Printing, February 1995
Tenth Printing, August 1996
Eleventh Printing, July 2000
Twelfth Printing, June 2005
Thirteenth Printing, October 2006
Fourteenth Printing, August 2007
Fifteenth Printing, September 2008
Sixteenth Printing, December 2009
Seventeenth Printing, July 2011
Eighteenth Printing, January 2013
Nineteenth Printing, December 2014

Distributed to the sewing market by:

BLUE FEATHER PRODUCTS, INC.
P.O. Box 2, Ashland OR 97520 USA
Tel: (800) 472-2487   Fax: (541) 482-2338
www.bluefeatherproducts.com

DESIGN ENTERPRISES OF S.F.
1007 Castro Street
San Francisco CA 94114

PRINTED IN U.S.A.

ACKNOWLEDGMENTS

A book such as this is never the work of one person. It is an accumulation of the thoughts, ideas, and knowledge of many people channeled onto the written page by the author.

I learned the principles of pattern drafting from Dr. Paul D. Reinhardt of the Drama Department at the University of Texas. This book is a result of both the content and the inspiration of his excellent teaching.

I wish to thank Harold H. Hart for publishing the first edition of this book. Since that printing I have had the opportunity of presenting these ideas to various pattern drafting classes. The most beneficial of these classes have been the ones I have taught at the San Francisco Community College Centers. I am deeply indebted to Dr. Alfred Azevedo for making them possible.

The people in these classes have improved this approach to pattern drafting immeasurably by their penetrating questions, by the wealth of personal knowledge they have shared, and by applying these techniques to the wide variety of their figure shapes.

Since this edition has been in manuscript form, I have had the help of many people in trying out the patterns, editing, and proofreading. In particular I wish to thank my wife Roxey, my parents Mr. and Mrs. Drummond J. McCunn, Stanley Sargent, and Gertrude II.

I am extremely grateful to Feather and John King of Blue Feather Products for keeping this book alive.

Fashion Dolls

In 2004, Bill Jones introduced me to the Fashion Dolls named Tyler, Alex, and Gene. These ¼ scale, adult-featured dolls are a perfect outlet for the techniques described in this book. If a pattern calls for a measurement in inches, such as a 1" standing collar, simply change the measurement to ¼". For more information about these dolls, visit my web site: Patterns-for-Fashion-Dolls.com.

TABLE OF CONTENTS

INTRODUCTION

Pattern drafting may seem like a complex and mystifying art, but basically it is a simple process. In essence, a two-dimensional piece of material is shaped and altered so that it will cover a three-dimensional body.

The first step in the drafting process is to take accurate measurements of the body to be covered. These measurements are then converted into basic patterns which fit the body closely. The basic patterns may then be adjusted, adapted, and altered to achieve different designs. Finally, subtle variations in the cut of a pattern may be made to give distinctive qualities to the finished shape.

Pattern drafting is only one part of the larger process of the design and construction of garments. The overall process will be described so that the specific role of pattern drafting may be better understood.

CLOTHING DESIGN

The conception of the design is the initial phase in clothing construction. The first consideration in design must be the function of the garment. Is it to be for a formal occasion, everyday wear, for work, or for play?

Once the purpose of the garment has been established, the specific design can be developed. The idea for the design may come from a style that was seen on the street, a garment viewed in a store window, a sketch in a clothing catalog, or from the imagination of the designer. Many different designs can be created by combining various standard sleeve and collar patterns with the basic body styles.

The idea for the design should then be converted into a sketch. This is an important step, because with the sketch the designer can evaluate the design. The sleeve may or may not be appropriate with the collar. The body may need to be adjusted to match the sleeve, and so forth.

Once the idea has been converted into a sketch, individual touches may be added. These individual touches may be used to compensate for any special qualities in the shape of the wearer so that the garment will be as flattering as possible. Or they may be used to increase the originality of the idea.

Next, material that is appropriate to the design must be purchased. In some cases a specific garment may be designed for material that has already been purchased. In this instance, the design should be adjusted to the nature of the material.

PATTERN DRAFTING

Pattern drafting is the first step in the process of turning a design conception into a reality. There are three basic elements to work with during drafting: 1) the sketch which shows the desired design, 2) the material which has been bought, 3) the measurements of the person who will wear the clothes.

Before drafting is started, such things as seam and dart placements and types of openings for the garment (i.e. lacings, buttons, hooks, eyes, zippers, etc.) must be determined. After this the material to be used must be examined for its properties of draping, weight, and flexibility. With these considerations in mind the actual drafting may be started.

The basic patterns are drafted on paper first. In the case of people who are sewing only for themselves and/or their families, these basic patterns may be drafted and carefully fit in muslin before any designs are considered. Custom designers, on the other hand, will have to draft the basic patterns for each new design according to the customer's measurements. Ready-to-wear designers will use the manufacturer's basic patterns which have been developed to fit as many people as possible.

These basic patterns are then altered to achieve the particular design desired. This design is then cut out of fabric, using wide seam allowances, and given a fitting.

FITTING

Fitting is a very important part of the pattern drafting process. Drafting establishes the basic location of the seams and the ·darts. The fitting establishes their exact location and makes it possible to compensate for the individual contours of the body being clothed. Before a garment is complete it should have at least two accurate fittings. Most of the adjustments occur during the first fitting which is usually pinned. The second fitting is done with the garment basted together and is a check on the first fitting.

Fitting sessions not only allow for correcting the patterns but they also provide an opportunity to devise subtle variations in the shape of the seams and the darts which will further enhance the design.

Once the garment has been carefully fitted it is ready for the final sewing operation.

This then is the basic sequence by which garments are created. Different circumstances may alter the specific steps followed and the order they come in but the concept is the same. The particular approach to pattern drafting described in this book has been developed to allow for maximum flexibility by showing that pattern drafting is simply a matter of altering fabric to fit the shapes of the body. Understanding pattern drafting in this way encourages creativity without sacrificing accuracy.

FABRIC AND THE BODY

Learning how to draft patterns is essentially a process of first understanding the contours of the human body and then learning how to shape flat fabric to fit these contours. With these two principles in mind individual problems and mistakes can be corrected. Not understanding these two concepts is the source of all errors in measuring, drafting, and fitting.

THE BODY

The body is a marvellous combination of many different shapes and curves. Most people are aware of the obvious shapes. Pattern drafters must become aware of all the shapes and of how movement affects these shapes.

There are so many different variations in the shapes of the body that it is impossible to describe them all in this introduction. The first part of this book is dedicated to an understanding of these contours. This is done by describing how to take measurements, draft the basic patterns, and fit the patterns to the body.

The important point is to start looking at the body now (Figure 1). The body has the three dimensions of height, width, and depth. It is a combination of continuously changing curves.

Look at each individual part of the body at a time comparing the front to the side to the back. There is the main torso. Connected to this are the arms, legs, and neck. Each of these joints becomes a special consideration in the pattern drafting procedure.

For instance, look at how the neck joins the body (Figure 1). The front view shows an abrupt angle as the neck meets the shoulder. The side view shows an almost straight line where the neck meets the front and the back of the body. The curve of the body is in one direction. The curve of the neck is in another.

The human body is exceedingly complex to describe. But by carefully looking at the body the most complex variations become immediately obvious. Similarly if any step in the measuring or pattern drafting procedure should become unclear, look at the body

THE BODY

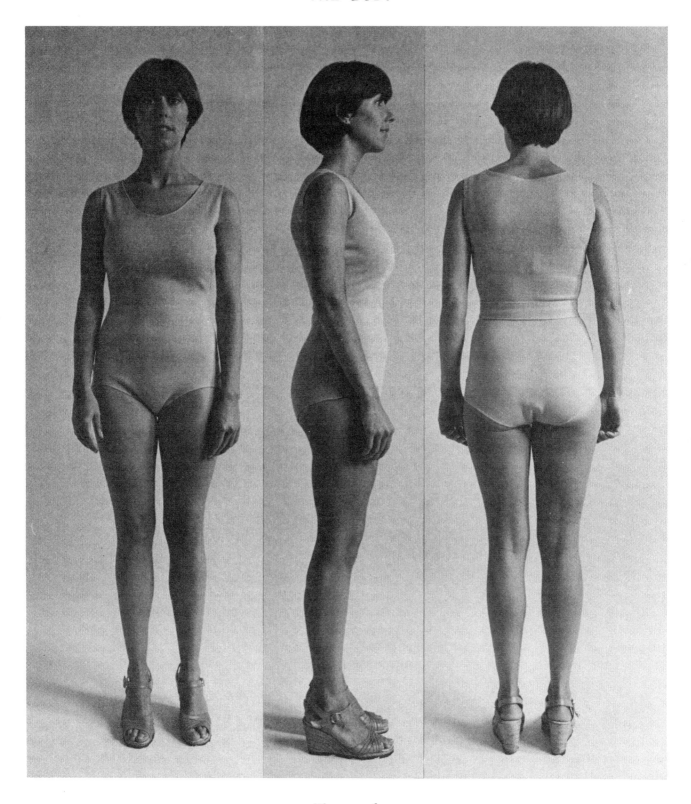

Figure 1

DART SHAPE

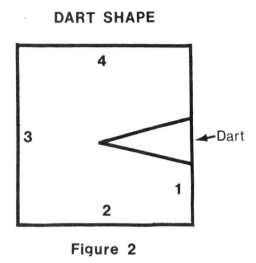

Figure 2

Darts

A dart is a "V" shaped wedge that is removed from the fabric so that the fabric will bend in two directions at one time. Paper may be used to demonstrate the basic idea of the dart.

Step 1. Take a piece of paper and draw a "V" shaped dart on it with the point near the center of the paper and the two legs running off one edge (Figure 2).

Step 2. Number the edges of the paper as in Figure 2.

Step 3. Cut out the dart and tape the two cut edges together (Figure 3).

Notice that the paper now bends in two directions. One bend in the paper follows the line of the dart from edge #1 to edge #3. The paper also bends from edge #2 to edge #4.

In fabric the wedge of the dart is normally sewn out rather than cut out but the principle of removing a wedge of the material and the resulting shape are the same.

TAPED DART

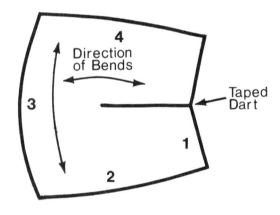

Figure 3

and see which of the contours is being used. It will make the whole process much easier.

SHAPING FABRIC

Fabric is essentially flat. It has the two dimensions of length and width. The third dimension of depth is negligible. It may be shaped to fit the three-dimensional human form just as paper may be used to gift wrap a box.

Studying paper is a good way of understanding how fabric responds to shaping. Paper is stiffer than fabric but it responds the same in all other ways.

For example, take a piece of paper and bend it from top to bottom. It bends easily. Now bend it from side to side. Once again it will bend easily in that one direction. But try bending it from top to bottom and from side to side at the same time. It cannot be done without wrinkling the paper.

Fabric, and paper, will bend smoothly in only one direction at a time. The contours of the body bend in many places in several directions at once. Therefore the fabric must be shaped to follow the contours of the body. The shaping devices in garment construction are darts and seams. Pattern drafting is the process of locating these darts and seams so that the fabric will lay flat where the body is flat and bend where the body bends. If the contours of the body are sucessfully followed there will be no unsightly bulges or wrinkles.

Seams

A seam joins two separate pieces of fabric together. Seams can affect the shape in three different ways.

1. Seams may be added to fabric without changing the shape of the fabric at all. For example, cut a piece of paper in half and tape it back together again. There is no change in the shape at all.

This is a decorative seam. It may be used to join together two pieces of different colored fabric as in patchwork quilts.

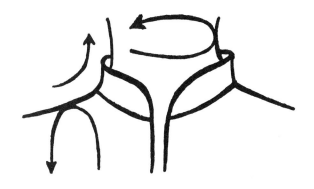

2. Seams may be used instead of darts to bend fabric in two directions at the same time. For example, take the piece of paper that was used for the dart. Cut from edge #3 to the point of the dart and tape it back together again.

This seam replaces the dart. The shape of the fabric is the same whether the dart or the seam is used to do the shaping.

3. Seams may be used to shape fabric so that it will bend in more than two directions at one time. Figure 4 illustrates a mandarin collar where fabric fits both the neck and the body smoothly. Notice how many different directions the fabric is going.

Putting darts and seams in fabric so it will fit the body is what pattern drafting is all about.

MANDARIN COLLAR

Figure 4

HOW TO USE THIS BOOK

This book has been developed to show when, where, why, and how to place darts and seams to obtain any desired design. It follows a series of steps. Each new step is based on the previous ones.

To benefit the most from this book, it is suggested that the reader try out each step as it is described. Also, the easiest patterns are presented first to give the reader a better understanding of the principles and techniques.

Measurements are described first. They are used to analyze the size and shape of the body. The measurements show the distances from given reference lines to basic seam locations.

Then, the basic patterns may be drawn by establishing the reference lines on paper and measuring the distances to the seam locations. This shows the three-dimensional shape of the body on two-dimensional paper.

Finally, the basic patterns are then transferred to cheap fabric, such as muslin, and checked for accuracy. If the measurements are taken accurately and the drafting is done correctly, there may be no adjustment necessary. On the other hand, not everyone is built the same. It may be necessary to

adjust the patterns to the individual shape of the wearer during the fitting.

The first part of this book will show the reader how to measure, draft, and fit these basic patterns. If you are developing these patterns for yourself, it is usually best to have someone help you with the measuring and the fitting. However, if you do not have someone who can help measure and fit you accurately, you will have to do this yourself. Special instructions have been included in each section on how to do this.

After the basic patterns have been drafted, these patterns may be changed to achieve any given style. Remember, the basic patterns are the shape of the body. All clothes are designed to fit certain parts of the body, hang from other parts, and be full in other areas. The basic patterns may be altered to achieve this.

The second section of this book shows techniques that can be used to alter the basic patterns. Most contemporary clothes are based on a few standard variations of sleeve, collar, and body patterns. Most of these variations are described in the section on pattern alterations.

The third section of this book shows how the various patterns may be put together to achieve different designs. Examples are given to show some of the many different variations that are possible.

One of the greatest thrills is to design, draft, sew, and wear your own creations.

To create an original design, start with a sketch. You do not have to be a great illustrator to be a good designer, so try it. The best way is to draw the desired design over a body silhouette. The silhouette will show the correct proportions of the body. Some body silhouettes are included at the end of this book. Other silhouettes may be acquired by tracing fashion illustrations and even photographs of models. Look for illustrations of swimsuits, underwear, and other tight fitting clothes to trace.

The final part of this book presents additional information to make designing, drafting, and sewing as rewarding as possible. There is a section which describes the way fabric relates to pattern drafting. Another chapter shows how to make a custom dress form accurately and inexpensively from the basic patterns. There is also a section on altering commercial patterns for fit.

QUARTER SCALE

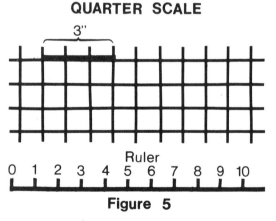

Figure 5

It will be easier to follow along with the book if the patterns are drafted to quarter scale first. Purchase a tablet of 8½" x 11" graph paper that is lined off in quarter inch squares. When a measurement calls for 3", for example, instead of measuring 3" you will count 3 squares (Figure 5). A quarter scale ruler, as shown above, will also be useful. This ruler may be made out of heavy paper.

Once the patterns are drafted to quarter scale it will be easier to make full size pat-

terns. The quarter scale patterns may also be used to practice pattern alteration.

The squared-off graph paper is suggested because pattern drafting frequently requires drawing parallel lines and right angles. The graph paper already indicates these.

These two drafting terms may be defined as follows:

Parallel lines are two lines that are the same distance away from each other for their entire length. They will never touch.

A right angle is a square corner. Two lines intersect forming a 90 degree angle. A plastic triangle may be used to help draw right angles, however, the corner of a piece of paper or of a book may also be used.

Another step that is frequently required in pattern drafting is to divide measurements into fourths and halves. To facilitate this a chart has been included at the very end of this book which automatically divides these measurements.

To use this chart and certain other pages in this book it may be helpful to "unbind" the book and mount it in a three ring binder.

To "unbind" the book open it to the middle, say around page 60. Pull it open at the spine. A sharp knife may be used to cut through the spine in this location. After it has been cut apart, pull off one page at a time. The pages will come off the same way paper may be torn off a tablet of scratch paper. Once the pages are removed they may be punched and put in a three ring binder.

REQUIRED MATERIALS
A Yardstick and Tape Measure
Pencil and Eraser
Right Angle Triangle
French Curve
Paper and Fabric Scissors
Large Sheets of Paper - Any large sheet of paper 24" or wider may be used for pattern drafting. Brown wrapping paper, news print, tracing paper, even old newspaper. The best paper to use, however, is the professional drafting paper that has dots every square inch. These dots make drawing parallel lines and right angles much easier. It is also semi-transparent for tracing other patterns. Some fabric stores carry this paper, especially stores specializing in knit fabric

CREATING THE BASIC PATTERNS

BASIC BODY CONTOURS AND LINES

BASIC REFERENCE LINES

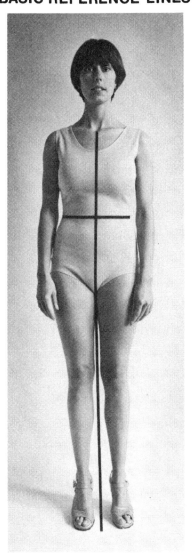

Figure 6

This approach to pattern drafting starts with the body. The basic lines of the body must be determined and understood if the patterns are going to be accurately drafted.

To draw the shape of the body on flat paper, a vertical reference line and a horizontal reference line must be established.

The most natural vertical line of the body is the spinal column. It is in the center of the body and it reaches from the top to the bottom of the torso. An imaginary line may extend it to the floor.

CENTER FRONT - The vertical line used for drafting patterns for the front part of the body will follow a line that is directly in front of the spinal column. It will be referred to as the Center Front (Figure 6).

CENTER BACK - The vertical line that follows the spinal column and is used for drafting patterns for the back will be referred to as the Center Back.

Once the vertical line is established, a horizontal line must be determined. The Waist will be the basic horizontal reference line used for this approach to pattern drafting.

WAIST - The Waist may be found by putting a string around the body and pulling it tight. This string must be kept parallel to the floor at all times.

Notice at the side of the body the Waist is between the bottom of the rib cage and the top of the hip bone. In men the distance between the rib cage and the hip bone is less than 1" but for women this distance is between 2" to 3". The Waist should be established within these limits at the most comfortable heighth for the wearer.

Important Note - The Waist used for measuring and drafting the basic patterns may or may not be the waist used in the final design. For example, men's pants are almost never designed to fit at the natural waist. They are 3" to 4" lower.

NECKLINE

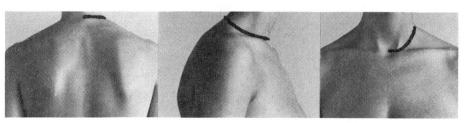

Figure 7

NECK PLANES

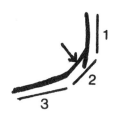

Figure 8

SHOULDER SEAM

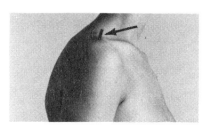

Figure 9

SHOULDER POINT

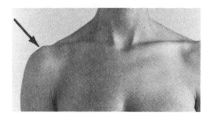

Figure 10

FINDING THE SHOULDER POINT

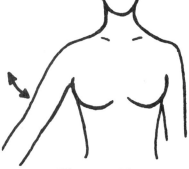

Figure 11

The next step is to determine the seam lines that will be used to measure, draft, and fit the basic patterns. These lines will follow the natural contours of the body. These contours are gradual curves. There are not definite points or lines to look for. Some locations, however, are better than others.

NECKLINE - The best way to determine the neckline in the back and to the side of the body is to put on a thin chain necklace or hold a string around the neck. This will follow the natural curves of the body (Figure 7).

Notice that the necklace or string at Center Back is just above a large vertebrae in the spinal column. Put a finger at this point and tip the head up and down. The large vertebrae does not move. It is a part of the body. The vertebrae just above it does move. It is a part of the neck.

The necklace then crosses over the shoulder at the base of the neck. In some cases this neck to shoulder area will have three planes (Figure 8). The necklace or string will cross the center of the middle plane.

From the shoulder the Neckline should follow the hollow between the neck and the collar bone around to the Center Front.

SHOULDER SEAM - The Shoulder Seam for the basic pattern is located on the top of the shoulder (Figure 9). It runs from the Neckline to the Sleeve Seam dividing the front of the body from the back of the body.

SHOULDER POINT - The Shoulder Point is where the Shoulder Seam meets the Sleeve Seam. It is the separation point between the body and the arm (Figure 10). It may be determined by raising the arm straight out from the side of the body (Figure 11). You can feel the bones in the arm move. The bones in the body do not move.

These are the most important lines of the body for the basic patterns. Establishing these lines correctly at this point will save much time and effort later in measuring, drafting, and fitting the basic patterns successfully.

MEASUREMENTS

Measurements are the foundation of pattern drafting. They determine the distances from the basic reference lines to the basic seam lines. And they are used to reconstruct the shape of the body on paper.

There are different ways to take measurements and also many different measurement charts. The pattern drafting instructions in this book are based on the specific measurements and the method of taking them described in this section.

The Measurement Chart is divided into two basic groups of measurements, Girth and Length. The Girth measurements are taken horizontally and most of them go around the entire circumference of the body. They should be taken parallel to the floor except where otherwise noted. Basically the Girth measurements give the size of the body.

Length measurements are taken vertically. They should be at right angles to the floor, except where noted otherwise. Their main purpose is to give the distances between the individual Girth measurements and also the distances from these measurements to the floor.

Several measurements will be taken from the same point on the body. These points should be clearly indicated so that the exact same location is used each time.

Waistline – It is very important to mark the waistline clearly by tying a string securely around the waist. Make sure the string is parallel to the floor.

Shoulder Seam/Neckline Point – This is the point where the Shoulder Seam intersects with the Neckline. Mark this in some way with either tape on the body or with a pin through the clothes. If the pin is used make sure the clothes do not shift as the measurements are taken.

Shoulder Point – The point where the Shoulder Seam meets the Sleeve Seam must also be clearly marked in the same manner.

The measurements should be taken snugly but not tightly (unless otherwise specified) with the subject standing in a relaxed, upright position. The measurements should be taken over any foundation garments that are going to be worn such as bras, corsets, or padding. They should not be taken over bulky clothing, such as knitted sweaters, as this will distort the measurements.

The approximate length of various measurements are given in parentheses. If the measurements, when they are taken, do not agree with those in parentheses, recheck them carefully.

The measurements of the Measurement Chart are all numbered. These numbers will be used throughout the book for easy reference.

MEASUREMENT CHART

GIRTH

BODY

1) Neck _____
2) NECK WIDTH _____
3) SHOULDER WIDTH _____

m 4) CHEST _____

w 5) UPPER CHEST _____

w 6) BUST, FULL _____

w 7) Bust, Front _____

w 8) Bust, Back _____

w 9) BUST TO BUST _____

w 10) Rib Cage _____

11) WAIST _____

ARM

12) BICEPS _____
13) Wrist _____
14) PALM _____

LEG

15) HIPS _____
16) THIGH _____
17) Leg Width _____
18) Knee _____

LENGTH

BODY

20) CENTER FRONT TO WAIST _____

w 21) Center Front to Rib Cage _____

w 22) Center Front to Knee _____

w 23) Center Front to Floor _____

w 24) SIDE FRONT TO BUST _____

25) SIDE FRONT TO WAIST _____

w 26) BUST TO SHOULDER _____

m 27) CENTER FRONT/WAIST TO SHOULDER _____

28) CENTER BACK _____

29) SIDE BACK _____

30) CENTER BACK/WAIST TO SHOULDER _____

31) ARMPIT TO WAIST _____

ARM

32) ARM LENGTH _____
33) Shoulder to Elbow _____
34) SLEEVE CAP _____

LEG

35) WAIST TO HIPS _____
36) Waist to Knee _____
37) WAIST TO FLOOR _____
38) INSEAM _____
39) Crotch Depth _____

ALL CAPITAL LETTERS indicates the basic pattern drafting measurements.
The Other Measurements are either used to double check the basic
measurements or for certain designs.

w - This indicates that these measurements are for women only.
m - This indicates that these measurements are for men only.

Girth Measurements

NECK WIDTH

Figure 12

BACK

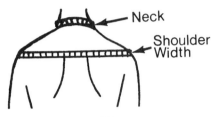

— Neck

Shoulder
— Width

Figure 13

FRONT

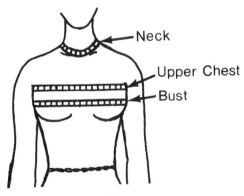

—Neck

—Upper Chest

—Bust

Figure 14

SIDE

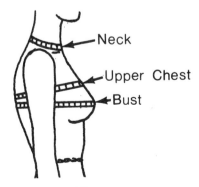

—Neck

—Upper Chest

—Bust

Figure 15

BODY

1) NECK - The first measurement is the neck circumference. It should be taken just over the large vertebrae at Center Back and over the collar bone in the front. The tape measure should follow the Neckline as it was previously described on page 14. The measurement should be snug but not tight.

2) NECK WIDTH - To take this measurement put a string around the neck and hold it down the front of the body (Figure 12). Measure from one side of the string to the other. (For women this measurement should be between 4" and 5" and for men it should be between 5" and 6".)

3) SHOULDER WIDTH - This measurement determines the distance between the left Shoulder Point and the right Shoulder Point. Be sure the tape measure is parallel to the ground. (The Shoulder Point that is referred to here and throughout the book is the Shoulder Point that was described on page 14.)

4) CHEST (Men only) - This measurement should be taken around the fullest part of the chest. The tape measure should cross over the shoulder blades in the back.

5) UPPER CHEST (Women only) - This is the circumference of the chest above the bust. It will not be possible to keep the tape measure parallel to the floor for this measurement because of the location of the arm. Take this measurement very snugly.

6) BUST, FULL (Women only) - The Bust measurement is taken around the fullest part of the bust. It will be over the shoulder blades in the back. Keep the tape measure parallel to the ground.

7) BUST, FRONT and
8) BUST, BACK (Women only) - The Bust measurement may be divided into a front and a back measurement. The difficulty in taking these two measurements is in determining exactly where both Side Seams should be located. It is best to take the Full Bust measurement starting at one Side Seam and placing the tape measure so that it goes around the front of the body then around the back. Hold the tape measure closed at the first Side Seam and locate the second Side Seam. The measurement found on the tape measure at this point will be the Front Bust Measurement. Subtract this from the Full Bust measurement to determine the Back Bust measurement.

FRONT

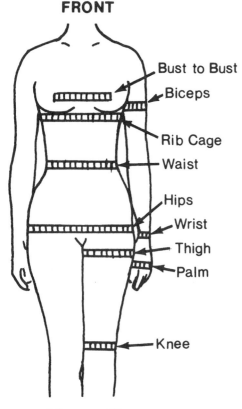

Figure 16

SIDE

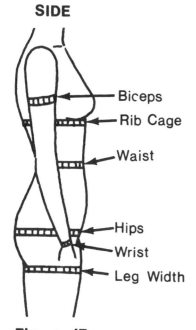

Figure 17

9) BUST TO BUST (Women only) - This measurement is taken from the apex of one bust to the apex of the other.

10) RIB CAGE (Women only) - The Rib Cage measurement is taken just below the bust. It does not go over the shoulder blades in back.

11) WAIST - The Waist should already have a string around it as described earlier. Take the Waist measurement directly over the string.

ARM

12) BICEPS - The Biceps measurement is made around the fullest part of the upper arm.

13) WRIST - The circumference of the Wrist just below the large wrist bone.

14) PALM - This is a circumference measurement taken around the largest part of the hand. This measurement is used to check finished patterns to make sure the hand will be able to get through the finished garment.

LEG

15) HIPS - The Hip measurement is taken over the fullest part of the hips. Look at the body from the side to determine this. This measurement should not be taken over wallets, checkbooks, or car keys. It is best to take measurement #35, the Waist to Hip measurement, while the tape is still around the hips for the Hip measurement.

16) THIGH - The circumference of the largest part of the leg near the crotch.

17) LEG WIDTH - The distance from the front of the leg to the back of the leg. This measurement is taken straight. It is best to take it with a ruler instead of a tape measure. (For women this distance is between 6" and 8" and for men it is between 7" and 9".)

18) KNEE - The circumference of the knee taken directly over the knee cap.

Length Measurements

FRONT

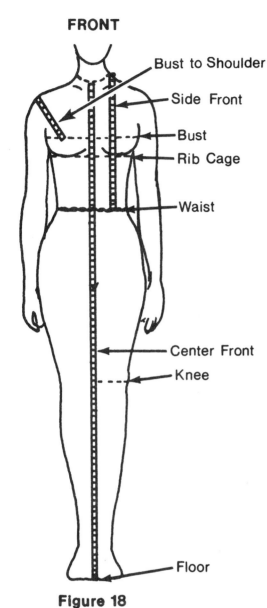

Figure 18

BACK

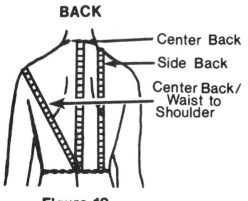

Figure 19

BODY

20) CENTER FRONT TO WAIST (Men & Women),
21) CENTER FRONT TO RIB CAGE (Women),
22) CENTER FRONT TO KNEE (Women), and
23) CENTER FRONT TO FLOOR (Women) - The Center Front measurements are taken down the middle of the front of the body starting at the hollow just above the two collar bones. These measurements should coincide with the locations of the earlier Girth measurements.

24) SIDE FRONT TO BUST (Women), and
25) SIDE FRONT TO WAIST (Men & Women) - The Side Front measurement starts from the point where the Shoulder Seam meets the Neckline as was described on page 14. It is taken down to the apex of the bust for women and down to the Waist for both men and women. The tape measure should be kept parallel to the Center Front while these measurements are being taken. (The Side Front to Waist measurement, #25, is usually 3" longer than the Center Front to Waist measurement #20.)

26) BUST TO SHOULDER (Women only) - The Bust to Shoulder measurement is taken diagonally from the apex of the bust to the Shoulder Point.

27) CENTER FRONT/WAIST TO SHOULDER (Men only) - This measurement is taken diagonally from the intersection of the Center Front and the Waist (the navel) to the Shoulder Point.

28) CENTER BACK - The Center Back measurement is taken from the top of the large vertebrae on the spinal column to the Waist. In other words from the Neckline to the Waist.

29) SIDE BACK - Start from the intersection of the Shoulder Seam and the Neckline and measure down to the Waist. The tape measure should be kept parallel to the Center Back. (The Side Back measurement and the Side Front measurement are usually the same length within 1" or so.) (The Side Back measurement is usually 1" longer than the Center Back measurement.)

30) CENTER BACK/WAIST TO SHOULDER - Measure diagonally from the intersection of the Center Back and the Waist to the Shoulder Point.

ARMPIT TO WAIST

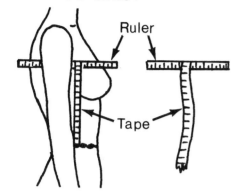

Figure 20

SIDE

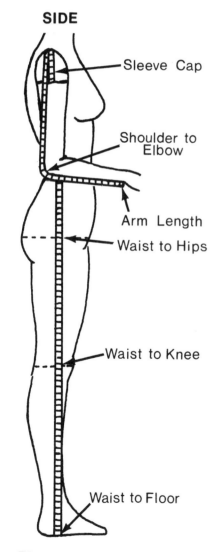

Figure 21

31) ARMPIT TO WAIST - This is taken down the side of the body from under the arm to the Waist. The best way to take this measurement is to attach the tape measure to the middle of a ruler (Figure 20). Place the ruler under the arm so that it is at a comfortable heighth, but not too low, then measure to the Waist.

ARM

32) ARM LENGTH - This measurement is taken from the Shoulder Point to the bottom of the large wrist bone. The arm should be bent at a right angle at the elbow. Make sure the tape measure goes over the back of the elbow.

33) SHOULDER TO ELBOW - Measure from the Shoulder Point to the elbow.

34) SLEEVE CAP - To measure the sleeve cap put a large rubber band or a piece of elastic that has been tied in a loop, over the arm. Slide the band to the highest point under the arm. With the arm down at the side of the body make sure the band is parallel to the floor. Now measure from the Shoulder Point to the band. This will be the Sleeve Cap measurement.

LEG

35) WAIST TO HIPS - This is the distance from the Waist to the fullest part of the hips. Take this measurement down the side of the body. It is best to take this measurement while the tape measure is still around the hips for measurement #15.

36) WAIST TO KNEE and
37) WAIST TO FLOOR - Measure down the side of the body from the Waist to the knee and the floor.

38) INSEAM - This is taken down the inside of the leg from the crotch to the floor. The person who is being measured should hold the tape measure in a comfortable position in the crotch.

39) CROTCH DEPTH - Have the person being measured sit erectly in a chair that has a flat seat to it. Measure down the side of the body from the Waist to the chair.

Measuring Yourself

The following instructions are given for those people who do not have anyone to help them take their measurements. Some measurements will not be difficult to take. They may be taken by following the instructions given previously. Other measurements will be a little more tricky because the body must not be twisted when these measurements are taken. Also the upper arms must be held down at the side of the body because raising the arms will distort the shoulders and all measurements taken to the shoulder locations.

You will need a mirror that is self standing. A full length mirror is best. You must be able to see your waist in the back.

The next step is to secure the end of your tape to the middle of a length of string, or twill tape about 5' to 6' long. If your tape measure has a metal plate on the end with a hole in it, thread the string through this. Otherwise pin the tape measure securely to the string or twill tape. This string will be used to hold the tape measure at the correct location while the measurement is taken. In this way there will be a minimum distortion of the body.

2) NECK WIDTH - Hold the string around the neck so that the left side is parallel to the right side (Figure 22). Measure between the two inside edges of the string.

3) SHOULDER WIDTH - Position the tape measure on the left Shoulder Point. Hold this end of the tape measure in place by holding the string in the left hand. One side of the string should be over the front of the body and the other side should be over the back of the body (Figure 23). Place the tape measure across the back to the right Shoulder Point. Hold this other end in place with the right hand. Both upper arms should be close to the sides of the body. Read the measurement at the right Shoulder Point in the mirror.

17) LEG WIDTH - This measurement must be taken from the front edge of the leg to the back edge of the leg with a straight ruler. Figure 24 shows how this measurement may be taken using a carpenter's square and a ruler. Another way to take this measurement is to place a ruler between the legs. Put a hand in back and adjust the ruler so that it just reaches the back of the leg. The measurement can then be read off of the front of the ruler.

NECK WIDTH

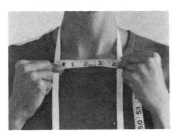

Figure 22

SHOULDER WIDTH

Figure 23

LEG WIDTH

Figure 24

SIDE FRONT

Figure 25

CENTER BACK

Figure 26

CENTER BACK/WAIST TO SHOULDER

Figure 27

ARM LENGTH

Figure 28

24 & 25) SIDE FRONT - The Side Front measurements may be taken by holding the end of the tape measure at the intersection of the Neckline and the Shoulder Seam by placing the string around the neck (Figure 25). Read the measurements in the mirror. The Waist measurement will be easier to read if the tape measure is threaded under the string that marks the Waist.

26) BUST TO SHOULDER (Women only) - Hold the end of the tape measure at the Shoulder Point with the string. Bring the tape measure over the apex of the bust and read the measurement in the mirror.

27) CENTER FRONT/WAIST TO SHOULDER (Men only) - Hold the end of the tape measure at the Shoulder Point with the string and measure to the navel.

28) CENTER BACK - Thread the tape measure under the string marking the Waist. Place the string holding the end of the tape measure around the neck. Adjust it so that the tape measure is directly over the spinal column in back. Hold the string down firmly in front. There is no need to adjust the tape measure up or down as the string will automatically hold it at the correct heighth. Read the measurement in the mirror (Figure 26). Or, with your free hand hold the tape measure with your thumb nail just below the waist string. Pull the tape measure free and read the measurement.

29) SIDE BACK - Thread the tape measure under the string marking the Waist. Place the string holding the tape measure around the neck and adjust the end of the tape measure to the intersection of the Neckline and the Shoulder Seam. Adjust the tape measure so that it is parallel to Center Back. Read the measurement at the Waist.

30) CENTER BACK/WAIST TO SHOULDER - Thread the tape measure under the Waist string. Locate the end of the tape measure at the Shoulder Point and hold it in place with the string (Figure 27). Adjust the tape measure so that it crosses the Center Back at the Waist. This measurement is taken diagonally. Read the measurement.

32 & 33) ARM LENGTH and SHOULDER TO ELBOW - Hold the tape measure at the Shoulder Point using the string. Run the tape measure down the arm and read the measurement at the wrist (Figure 28). Read the Shoulder to Elbow measurement in the mirror.

WAIST TO KNEE

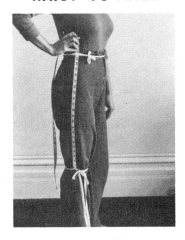

Figure 29

WAIST TO FLOOR

Figure 30

CROTCH DEPTH

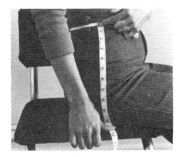

Figure 31

35) WAIST TO HIPS - Tie the string holding the tape measure around the fullest part of the hips. Position the tape measure at the side of the body. Check the location of the tape measure by looking in the mirror at the side of the body. Measure up to the Waist.

36) WAIST TO KNEE - Tie the string holding the tape measure at the knee and measure up to the Waist (Figure 29).

37) WAIST TO FLOOR - With the string hold the tape measure just at the outside edge of the foot. Measure up to the Waist (Figure 30).

38) INSEAM - Hold the end of the tape measure just at the inside edge of the foot using the string. Measure up to the crotch.

39) CROTCH DEPTH - Sit on a chair with a flat hard seat. Measure from the Waist to the chair (Figure 31).

FABRIC GRAIN LINES

Fabric grain lines are what make patterns work or not work when the patterns are cut out of fabric. Fabric has horizontal and vertical lines just as the body has horizontal and vertical lines. Pattern drafting must match the lines of the body to the lines of the fabric to ensure the best possible fit for the finished garment.

Woven fabric starts with vertical threads on a loom. All of these vertical threads are held parallel to each other. A series of horizontal threads is woven between the vertical threads. The two sets of threads are at perfect right angles to each other. The direction of the threads is the direction of the grain of the fabric. There is both a horizontal grain and a vertical grain.

The way to determine the grain of a given piece of fabric is to select a single thread and follow it for its entire length. Or a single thread may be pulled out of the fabric leaving an empty space between the adjacent threads.

As the fabric is shaped to fit the contours of the body it will not always be possible to keep the grain lines in vertical and horizontal directions. Therefore the most important locations for the grain lines to remain horizontal and vertical must be determined for each pattern piece. The descriptions for the basic patterns will show where the best locations are for fitted garments.

EASE

Patterns may not be made to the exact size of the body because they would be uncomfortable and they would restrict movement. The extra width added to the body measurements to create the patterns is called Ease.

There are two kinds of Ease. The first is Fitting Ease. This is the number of inches that must be added to the basic patterns to make them wearable. The second kind of ease is Design Ease. This is the amount that patterns are expanded to create the desired fullness in a given design.

Ease is a variable factor. It must be adjusted to the individual tastes of the person wearing the clothes and/or the designer. The amounts of Ease given in this book are only intended to be a starting point for individual preference.

THE BASIC SKIRT

The basic skirt pattern will be primarily of interest to people making women's clothes. However, people specializing in men's clothes should read this section also because the basic concepts and techniques presented here will apply to all subsequent patterns. The skirt pattern is presented first because it is the simplest of all the basic patterns.

The Body and the Skirt

The basic fitted skirt will be designed to fit the Waist to Hip region closely. From the hips the skirt will hang down to the desired hem.

The Center Front and the Center Back lines will be the basic vertical reference lines for the skirt pattern. These lines will follow the vertical grain of the fabric.

The Hip line will be the line that follows the horizontal grain of the fabric. If the grain of the fabric is kept parallel to the ground at this point the skirt will hang correctly (Figure 32). If the grain is not parallel to the ground around the entire body, the skirt will pitch forward, backwards, or side ways.

To keep the Hip line parallel to the ground the skirt must be carefully shaped to follow the contours of the body from the Hips to the Waist. The skirt will actually be held up by the Waist. If the Waist is incorrectly adjusted the Hip line will not stay parallel to the ground.

SKIRT GRAIN LINES

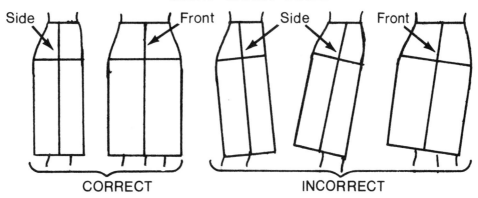

CORRECT   INCORRECT

Figure 32

WAIST TO HIPS

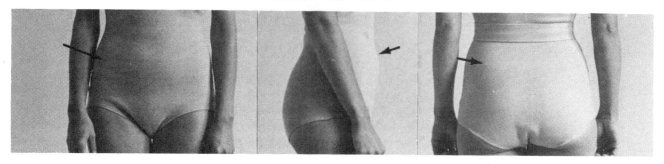

Figure 33

CURVE AT HIP

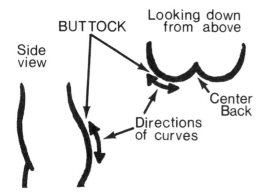

Figure 34

CURVE AT SIDE

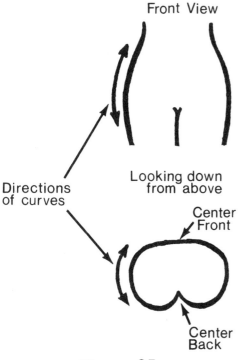

Figure 35

WAIST TO HIPS - Look at this area of the body carefully (Figure 33). The side view clearly shows that from the Waist the body curves out to the Hips. If you were to look straight down at the hips you would see that the hips also curve around from the Center Back to the side of the body (Figure 34). The body curves in two directions at the hips. This means that if the fabric is to fit the body in this area it must have a dart (or a seam).

Another obvious set of curves is at the side of the body (Figure 35). The body curves out from the Waist down to the Hips. From a top view you may see it also curves around from Center Front to Center Back. Another dart or seam must be placed here if the fabric is to fit smoothly.

These two shapes at the back and the side are similar in women and men except that men do not have as much of a curve from the Waist to the Hips at the side of the body as women do.

Women have three other areas for shaping that are less obvious. Since not all women are shaped the same in these areas either, each skirt should be shaped to fit the individual contours of the wearer.

1) Tummy to Waist - Some women have an indentation above the tummy in to the Waist. This may require a dart from 3" to 4" out from the Center Front towards the Side Seam. This contour is indicated in Figure 33 by the arrow on the side view.

2) Pelvic Bone - Some women have a distinct contour where the pelvic bone is located. This may require a dart depending on the degree the Waist is indented. This contour is indicated by the arrow on the front view in Figure 33.

3) High Hip - Some women have a high hip in the back near the side of the body. This may require an additional dart. This contour is indicated by an arrow on the back view of Figure 33.

HIP FULLNESS

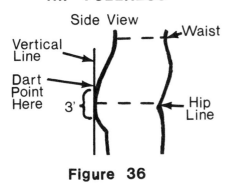

Figure 36

Important Note - Looking at the side of the body you can see that the fullest part of the hips is a gradual curve. If a straight vertical line is drawn at this point the hips would coincide with it for about 3" of its length (Figure 36). This means that the Hip line could be established anywhere in this area. The recommended area is in the middle of the fullness. The hip dart will have to stop at the top of this fullness. Check the Waist to Hip measurement (#35) to establish the correct location for this Hip line.

The Skirt Pattern

The basic skirt pattern will be drafted to fit one-fourth of the body. There will be a side seam dividing the front from the back. And there will be a Center Front/Center Back line dividing the left side from the right side. Asymmetrical bodies are best adjusted for in a fitting.

The difference between the front skirt pattern and the back skirt pattern will be in the length, size, and location of the darts and the shaping of the side seams. These factors will be determined in a fitting because it is too difficult to measure accurately for the exact shape of these contours of the body. Standard dart sizes and locations will not be drafted in because they apply only to standard shaped bodies.

The basic pattern drafted for one-fourth the skirt will be transferred to the fabric twice. First it will be used to cut out the front section, then it will be used to cut out the back section.

THE SKIRT PATTERN AND THE BODY

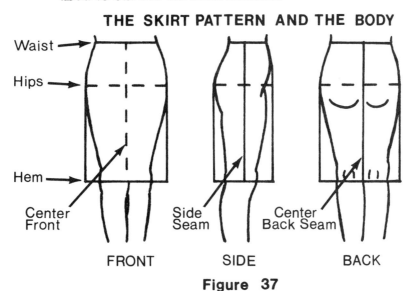

Figure 37

Measurements:

#36) Waist to Knee _____

#35) Waist to Hips _____

#15) Hips _____

#11) Waist _____

BASIC REFERENCE LINES

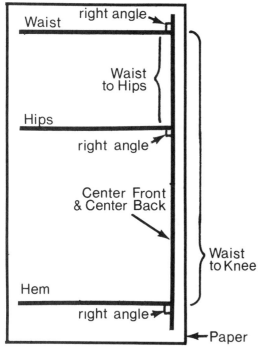

Figure 38

THE BASIC REFERENCE LINES

Step 1. Cut out a piece of paper that is at least 4" wider than one-fourth the Hip measurement (#15). It should also be 5" longer than the Waist to Knee measurement (#36), or the desired Waist to Hem length.

Step 2. Draw a vertical line 1" in from the edge of the paper (Figure 38). Mark off the Waist to Knee measurement (#36) on this line. You may substitute a different Waist to Hem measurement here if you wish. This line is the Center Front/Center Back line of the skirt.

Step 3. At the top of the Waist to Knee length draw a line at right angles to the Center Front/Center Back line. This will be the Waist line.

Step 4. At the bottom of the Waist to Knee length draw another line at right angles to the Center Front/Center Back line. This is the Hem line.

Step 5. Measure down from the Waist line on the Center Front/Center Back line the Waist to Hip measurement (#35). At this point draw another line at right angles to the Center Front/Center Back line. This is the Hip line.

This establishes the basic reference lines for the skirt pattern. Measurements may now be made from the Center Front/Center Back line to establish the location of the Side Seam.

THE SIDE SEAM

Step 6. Measure out from the Center Front/Center Back line 1/2" plus one-fourth of the Hip measurement (#15) on the Waist, Hip, and Hem lines making a mark on each line. These will be the Side Hip points (Figure 39).

The Hip measurement is divided into fourths because the pattern is to cover one-fourth of the body. 1/2" is added to this measurement to allow for ease of movement. (Do not forget the chart at the end of the book for dividing measurements.)

Step 7. On the Waist line mark off one-fourth of the Waist measurement (#11). This will be the Side Waist mark.

SIDE SEAM

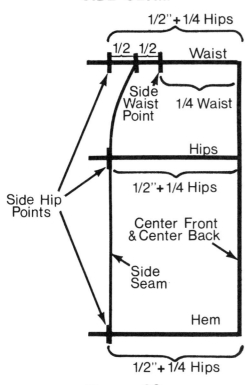

Figure 39

SEAM ALLOWANCES

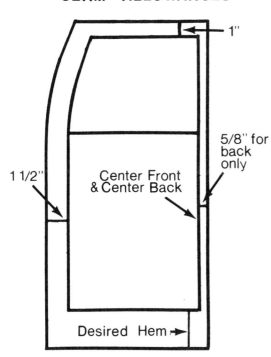

Figure 40

Step 8. To shape the Side Seam find a point on the Waist line that is half way between the Side Waist point and the Side Hip point. The Side Seam will start here. Curve this out and down toward the Side Hip point on the Hip line.

This line should curve out the most in the top 3" of the Side Seam because women's bodies have the greatest amount of curve from the Waist to the hip bone on the side of the body.

The Side Seam is not curved all the way into the Waist measurement because some allowance must be left in the fabric for the darts. Only part of the curve of the body is at the side. The rest is in the front and the back and this will be shaped in with darts.

Step 9. From the Side Hip point on the Hip line continue the Side Seam straight down to the Side Hip point on the Hem line.

Important Note - Patterns are described in this book in terms of seam lines rather than seam allowance lines because the seam lines determine the shape of the garment. Seam allowances are always added to the patterns as the last step. These seam allowances should be classified as sewing allowances or fitting and design allowances. A 5/8" seam allowance is not wide enough to make any practical adjustment to a garment. It should only be used on seam lines that are not going to be adjusted in any way.

SEAM ALLOWANCES

Step 10. Normally in a skirt of this type the Front section will be out of a single piece of fabric. The Center Front line will therefore be a fold line. There will be no seam allowances added here. The Center Back, on the other hand, is usually a seam. A 5/8" sewing allowance may be added to Center Back. (The allowance for the Center Back may be added to the pattern and when the Center Front section is cut out simply fold the seam allowance under.)

The Side Seam should have a 1 1/2" fitting and design allowance added. The Waist line should have a 1" fitting allowance (Figure 40).

FITTING PROCEDURES

After the paper patterns have been drafted the lines must be transfered to fabric for a fitting. Muslin or any inexpensive woven fabric may be used for this purpose. Do not, however, use loosely woven fabrics because the vertical and horizontal grain lines will not remain at right angles making an accurate fitting impossible.

Transfer the sewing lines and the basic reference lines from the paper pattern to the fabric. Be sure the basic reference lines follow the grain lines in the fabric.

The lines may be transferred with a tracing wheel and tracing paper. Or if the lines on the paper pattern are dark enough the fabric may simply be placed on top of the patterns and the lines can then be traced. A black felt tip marker is best for drawing these lines.

After the fabric has been marked and cut out it is ready for a fitting. It is always best to do two fittings for the basic patterns. The first fitting may be done by pinning the garment together as the fitting progresses. Do all of the fitting for only one-half of the body.

Once the first fitting has been completed the garment may be taken off. The pin locations must be carefully marked. Do not forget to mark both sides of the pinning. A red felt tip marker will help to make these corrections distinctive. At each seam place one pin at right angles to the seam line. Mark each side of the fabric where this pin is. This mark can then be used to align the seams for the next fitting.

When all of the pin locations have been marked take the garment apart. Use a ruler and a french curve to smooth out the lines. Remember the body is a series of gradual curves. There should be no abrupt angles. If certain pin marks do not align with the others ignore them.

Transfer the fitting corrections from the fitted side to the side that was not fitted. Then baste the garment together either by hand or machine and try it on for a second fitting. During the second fitting adjustments may be made for any asymmetrical qualities.

Once the garment has been carefully checked for correct fit it should be taken apart and the corrections transfered back to the paper patterns. If the corrections are extensive a fresh piece of paper may be necessary.

Fitting the Skirt

FITTING AT CENTER BACK

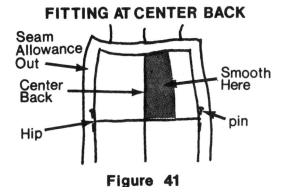

Figure 41

FITTING THE SIDE

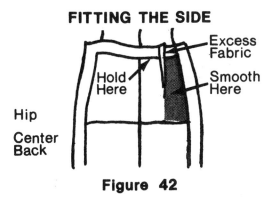

Figure 42

DART LOCATION

Buttock looking down from above

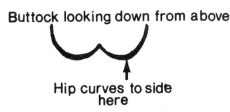

Hip curves to side here

Figure 43

DART LENGTH

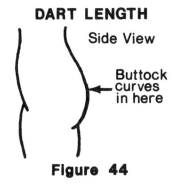

Figure 44

After the skirt has been drafted it may now be cut out of muslin for a fitting.

Step 1. Put the skirt around the person who is to wear it and pin the Side Seams together at the Hip line. Pin the skirt snugly at this time so that it will stay up on its own. Make sure the Hip line on the fabric is parallel to the floor. Check to make sure the Center Front and Center Back lines are following the body properly.

The ease originally allowed in the pattern for movement has been temporarily removed by this step. It will be added back later.

Step 2. Start at the Center Back and smooth the fabric up from the Hip line to the Waist (Figure 41). Hold this in place and smooth the fabric on the side of the buttock from the Hip line to the Waist (Figure 42). Pin out the excess fabric at the Waist.

Step 3. Look down at the top of the buttock and determine where the curve breaks from Center Back towards the side (Figure 43). Mark that point at the Hip line.

Step 4. Look at the side of the body and determine where the buttock starts to curve in to the Waist (Figure 44). Mark this heighth with a pin. Combine the horizontal line of this pin with the vertical line of the pin from Step 3 to determine the point of the dart.

The darts during the first fitting should only be marked with one pin showing the size of the dart at the Waist and one pin showing the point of the dart. This second pin should be placed horizontally catching only enough threads to clearly indicate the point of the dart.

Step 5. Shape the darts for the other contours of the body as they were described earlier: the high hip, the tummy, and the pelvic bone as necessary. Each time the fabric should be smoothed out starting at the center side of the body then the side of the countour should be shaped. The excess is pinned out at the waist and the point of the dart is established.

Remember that not every woman's body is going to require all four darts. Some women may only require the dart for the buttock. Others may require an additional front dart. Some women may need all four darts. Look for the locations on the body where the contours change in both a horizontal direction and a vertical direction at the same time.

DART FOLD

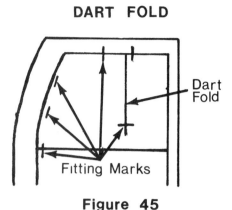

Figure 45

DART DIRECTION

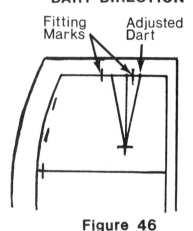

Figure 46

Step 6. After all the darts have been established, shape the Side Seam. Smooth the front toward the back and the back toward the front. The Side Seam should hang straight down the body. It should divide the distance between the front of the body and the back of the body equally in half.

Step 7. Check to make sure the Center Front, Center Back, and Hip lines are in their correct locations. Tie a string around the Waist. Make sure it is parallel to the floor. Mark the Waist on the fabric by drawing a line just above the string with a felt tip marker.

Step 8. Take the skirt off. Mark the pin locations on both sides of the darts and seams and remove the pins.

Step 9. Find the point of the buttock dart on the back of the skirt. Draw a line from this point to the Waist keeping the line parallel to the Center Back line (Figure 45). This will be the Center Fold line of the dart.

Step 10. Measure the pinned out dart width for the buttock dart at the Waist line. Divide this dart width so that half of the dart width is on one side of the Center Fold line and the other half is on the other side (Figure 46).

This positions the dart for the most pleasing position.

Step 11. Procede to redraw the other darts in the same manner.

Keep the darts separated from each other and from the Side Seam, Center Back, and Center Front by at least 2 1/2" to 3" for the best appearance.

Step 12. Add the ease back in at the Side Seam and continue with the fitting as was described in the section on Fitting Procedures on page 30.

THE BASIC PANTS

The basic pants pattern may be styled into many different variations without using the pattern alteration techniques described later in this book. Some of these styling suggestions are included at the end of this section. You may wish to procede from the pants pattern to the descriptions of waistbands and pockets in order to create functional garments right away.

The Body and the Pants

The basic pants pattern, like the basic skirt pattern, will be designed to fit the Waist to Hip region closely. From there it will hang down to the floor. The Side Seam will be the same as in the skirt pattern but the Center Front and the Center Back must be divided from the crotch down to form the Inseam (Figure 47).

The basic vertical reference line for the pants pattern will have to follow the center of the leg rather than the center of the body. The basic horizontal line will once again be the Hip line.

The same techniques may be used to draft pants for men and women. The patterns will then be individualized to the shape of the wearer with the dart sizes and locations and with the shaping of the Side Seam.

THE PANTS PATTERN AND THE BODY

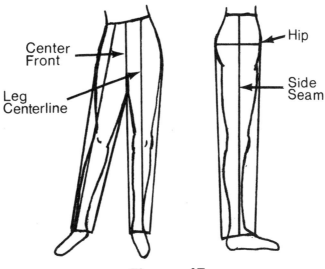

Center Front

Leg Centerline

Hip

Side Seam

Figure 47

The Front Pants Pattern

Measurements:

#37) Waist to Floor _____

#38) Inseam _____

#39) Crotch Depth _____

#16) Thigh _____

#11) Waist _____

#35) Waist to Hips _____

#15) Hips _____

#36) Waist to Knee _____

#17) Leg Width _____

LEG REFERENCE LINES

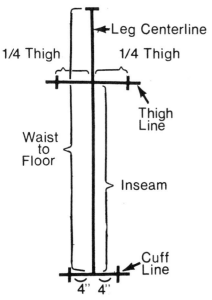

Figure 48

The leg portion of the pants will be drafted first from the crotch to the floor. Then the shape of the torso from the crotch to the Waist will be added.

THE BASIC REFERENCE LINES - LEG

Step 1. Draw a vertical line of the Waist to Floor length (#37). This is the Leg Centerline which divides most of the measurements for the pants pattern in half (Figure 48).

Step 2. At the bottom of this line draw a line at right angles to it. Mark off 4" on either side of the Leg Centerline. This is the Cuff line.
The 4" width used here is set as a standard measurement to show the general taper of the leg. The pants cannot fit the leg tightly at this point because there must be an allowance for getting the foot through the finished garment.

Step 3. Mark the Inseam length (#38) on the Leg Centerline measuring up from the Cuff line. Draw a line at right angles to the Leg Centerline at this point. This is the Thigh line.

Optional - The Crotch Depth measurement (#39) may be used to double check the height of the Thigh line. Measure down from the Waist the Crotch Depth measurement (#39). This should coincide with the Thigh line. If it does not coincide, recheck both measurements carefully. If there is still a disparity, use the higher of the two levels. The correct height can then be verified in a fitting.

Step 4. Mark off one-fourth of the Thigh measurement (#16) on the Thigh line on either side of the Leg Centerline.
The Leg Girth measurements are divided in half for the front section of the leg pattern. These measurements are then bisected by the Leg Centerline, hence the one-fourth measurement.

Now that the leg section of the pants has been drafted in, the torso portion may be added.

TORSO REFERENCE LINES

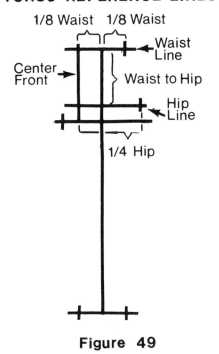

Figure 49

SEAM LINES

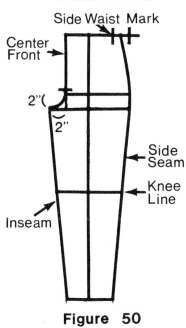

Figure 50

THE BASIC REFERENCE LINES - TORSO

Step 5. Draw a line at right angles to the top of the Leg Centerline (Figure 49). This is the Waist line.

Step 6. Measure down the Leg Centerline the Waist to Hip measurement (#35) and draw another line at right angles to the Leg Centerline. This is the Hip line.

Step 7. Mark off one-eighth of the Waist measurement (#11) on both sides of the Leg Centerline at the Waist. Draw a line from the left Waist mark to the Thigh line keeping it parallel to the Leg Centerline. This line is the Center Front line of the pants.

The Waist measurement is divided into eighths because this section of the pants is for one-fourth of the body. The Leg Centerline divides this measurement in half, therefore one-eighth of the total Waist measurement.

Step 8. Mark off one-fourth of the Hip measurement (#15) on the Hip line measuring out from the Center Front line.

Notice that the Hip measurement is taken from the Center Front line rather than the Leg Centerline as the other measurements were.

THE SEAM LINES

Step 9. Measure from the Center Front line to the left mark on the Thigh line (Figure 50). This distance should be 1 3/4" to 2". If it is less than this, extend the Thigh line out to 1 3/4" for women and 2" for men.

Step 10. Measure up 2" from the Thigh line on the Center Front line. From this point curve in the Front Crotch curve to the left mark on the Thigh line. This curve should be almost a quarter of a circle in shape.

Step 11. Draw a line straight down from the left mark on the Thigh line to the left mark on the Cuff line. This is the Inseam.

Step 12. On the Waist line find the mark that is one-fourth the Waist measurement from Center Front. This is the Side Waist mark.

For men the Side Seam will start from this point.

For women make a mark on the Waist line that is one-fourth the Hip measurement from Center Front. The Side Seam for women will start half way between this point and the Side Waist point just as it did for the skirt pattern.

CROTCH LENGTH

Standing   Sitting

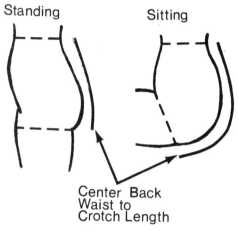

Center Back
Waist to
Crotch Length

Figure 51

BACK REFERENCE LINES

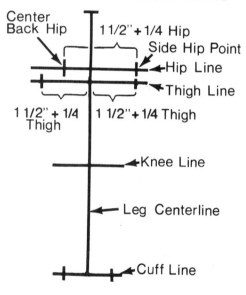

Center
Back Hip   1 1/2"+1/4 Hip
                            Side Hip Point
                        ←Hip Line
                        ←Thigh Line

1 1/2"+1/4   1 1/2"+1/4 Thigh
Thigh

←Knee Line

←Leg Centerline

←Cuff Line

Figure 52

RAISED HIP LINE

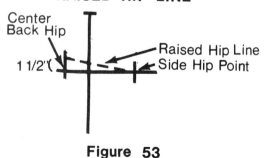

Center
Back Hip
                    Raised Hip Line
1 1/2"   Side Hip Point

Figure 53

Step 13. Draw in the Side Seam starting from the appropriate mark described in Step 12. Curve the Side Seam out from the Waist to the mark on the right side of the Hip line. Then extend the Side Seam straight down from the Hip to the mark on the right side of the Cuff line. If the mark on the Thigh line is to the right of the Side Seam, curve the Side Seam out to this mark then down to the Cuff line.

The pants as they are now drafted show the basic taper of the leg. For more stylish pants the height of the knee must be established. The pants may then be styled from this point. Styling suggestions will be given at the end of this section.

Step 14. Measure down the Leg Centerline the Waist to Knee length (#36). Draw a line at right angles to the Leg Centerline at this point.

The Back Pants Pattern

The back pants pattern is different from the front pants pattern in two ways. First, ease will be added to the back measurements to allow for movement of the body. Secondly, the back pattern must be adjusted for sitting.

Look at Figure 51. The distance from the Waist to the crotch is longer when a person is sitting than when a person is standing. This must be compensated for by adding a "hinge" to the back patterns at the Hip line.

The back pattern may be drafted by tracing the front pattern making the following adjustments as the pattern progresses.

THE BASIC REFERENCE LINES

Step 1. Trace the Leg Centerline, Hip line, Thigh line, Knee line, and Cuff line of the front pattern (Figure 52). Trace the two marks at the Cuff line for the Inseam and the Side Seam. Include a mark on the Hip line where the Center Front line coincides with the front Hip line. This mark is the Center Back Hip point.

The tracing may be made by placing semi-transparent paper on top of the front pants pattern. Or by placing the front pants pattern on top of another sheet of paper and transferring the marks with a tracing wheel and tracing paper.

Step 2. On the Thigh line mark off 1 1/2" plus one-fourth of the Thigh measurement to either side of the Leg Centerline.

PIVOTED PATTERNS

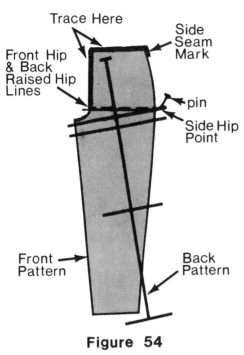

Figure 54

SEAM LINES

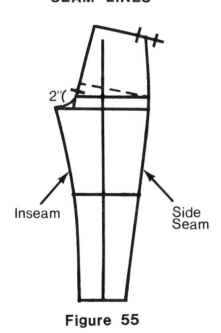

Figure 55

Step 3. For Men: Measure out from the Center Back Hip point on the Hip line 2" plus one-fourth of the Hip measurement (#15). This mark is the Side Hip point.

For Women: Measure out from the Center Back Hip point on the Hip line 1 1/2" plus one-fourth of the Hip measurement (#15). This mark is the Side Hip point.

Step 4. For Men: Measure straight up from the Center Back Hip point 2" and make a mark. Connect this point to the Side Hip point with a dotted line. This is the Raised Hip line.

For Women: Measure straight up from the Center Back Hip point 1 1/2" and make a mark. Connect this point to the Side Hip point with a dotted line. This is the Raised Hip line (Figure 53).

The Raised Hip line creates the "hinge" at Center Back that provides the extra fabric required for sitting.

THE PIVOT

Step 5. Keep the back and front patterns aligned at the Leg Centerline and the Hip line. Put a pin through both patterns at the back Side Hip point. Pivot the patterns at the pin so that the front Hip line coincides with the back Raised Hip line (Figure 54).

Step 6. Trace the Center Front line and the Waist line from the front pattern onto the back pattern. Also mark the location of the front Side Seam at the Waist on the back Waist line.

THE SEAM LINES

Step 7. Remove the back pattern from the front pattern.

For Women: Start drawing in the back Side Seam from the point established in Step 6 (Figure 55). Curve the Side Seam out to the Side Hip point and down to the mark on the Cuff line.

For Men: Find the point on the back Waist line where the front Side Seam started (Step 6). Measure out on the Waist line from this point 2" and draw in the Side Seam starting from this new point. Curve it to the Side Hip point and down to the Cuff line.

The 2" added at the back Waist line is a dart allowance for the buttock dart.

Step 8. Extend the Center Back line straight down to the Thigh line. Measure up from the Thigh line 2" and make a mark. From this point curve the back Crotch Curve out to the left mark on the Thigh line.

CROTCH CURVE

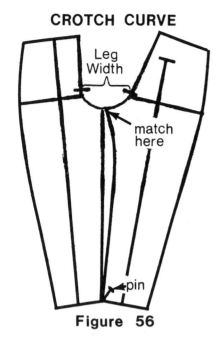

Figure 56

CROTCH WIDTH

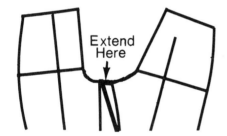

Figure 57

SIDE SEAMS

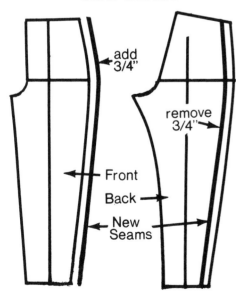

Figure 58

Step 9. Draw in the Inseam from the left mark on the Thigh line to the left mark on the Cuff line. The Inseam should curve in at the top as is illustrated in Figure 55.

The pattern as it is now drafted may fit with no problem at all. However, some body shapes will require an additional check to make sure the Crotch Curve will provide a comfortable fit.

THE CROTCH CURVE

Step 10. Place the front and the back pants pattern so that the Inseams touch at the top and the bottom as is illustrated in Figure 56.

Step 11. Put a pin through the back Inseam and the front Inseam at the Cuff lines. This pin is to act as a pivot for the patterns.

Step 12. Pivot the patterns so that the front Inseam at the Thigh line touches the back Inseam at the Thigh line.

Step 13. Measure from the top of the front Crotch Curve to the top of the back Crotch curve. This measurement should be the Leg Width length (#17).

Step 14. If it is not the Leg Width measurement, pivot the patterns until this measurement is reached.

Step 15. Shorten or lengthen the back Crotch Curve and the back Inseam so that they coincide with the front Crotch Curve and the front Inseam (Figure 57).

The following chart gives approximate Leg Width measurements for men and women.

LEG WIDTH

	Small	Medium	Large
Men	6"	7-8"	9"
Women	6"	7"	8"

WOMEN'S SIDE SEAMS

The following adjustment may be made to the Side Seam on women's pants either in a fitting or at this time. This adjustment will generally give the pants a more pleasing appearance.

Step 16. Move the front Side Seam out 3/4" for its entire length (Figure 58). Move the back Side Seam in 3/4" for its entire length.

INSEAM LENGTH

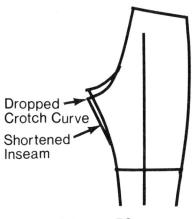

Dropped →
Crotch Curve

Shortened ˎ
Inseam

Figure 59

INSEAM LENGTH

Step 17. On the front pattern measure the
Inseam from the knee to the crotch. Next measure
the curved Inseam of the back pattern from the knee
to the crotch. If the back pattern is longer, due to
the curved seam, drop the back Crotch Curve to the
correct length (Figure 59). Do not shorten the
width of the Crotch Curve. Just drop the height.

The patterns as they are now drafted may be
fitted and then used as a basic pattern to create other
styles. Or, if you wish, the basic pants patterns
may be styled first then fitted. Styling suggestions
follow the section on fitting.

SEAM ALLOWANCES

The following seam allowances should be added
before the patterns are cut out for a fitting. The
Side Seam and the Inseam should have a 1 1/2"
fitting and design allowance. The Waist should have
a 1" fitting allowance. The Center Front, Crotch
Curve, and Center Back should have a 5/8" sewing
allowance. A larger seam allowance on the Crotch
Curve will make an accurate fitting impossible.

Fitting the Pants

The pants pattern is now ready to be cut out of
muslin and fitted. The pattern drafting approach
described here in combination with the methods used
to check the patterns reduce fitting time to a minimum.
However, individual figures vary and it will be
necessary to check the Crotch Curve and shape the
Waist to Hip region to the particular shape of the
wearer.

Each seam in the pants has its own particular
function in making pants fit well. It is important to
understand these functions not only for fitting the
basic patterns but also for styling and designing any
pants pattern.

PANT SEAMS

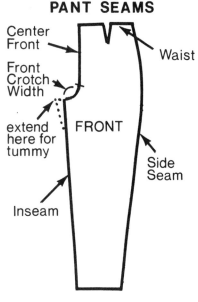

Figure 60

FRONT CROTCH WIDTH

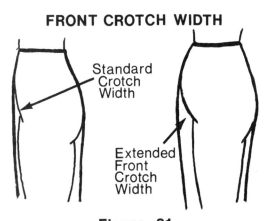

Figure 61

Waist - The Waist must fit the body closely. The pants will actually hang from the Waist. It must be adjusted, as with the skirt, so that the pants fall correctly pitching neither sideways, forwards, or backwards.

Side Seam - The Side Seam is responsible for the overall fit of the pants. It may be adjusted so that the pants are either close fitting or loose.

Center Front - The Center Front seam should follow the Center Front of the body. It should follow the grain of the fabric. The Center Front is normally a straight seam not a shaped seam.

Center Back - This seam is slightly off the grain of the fabric to provide give at the back for sitting. It is normally straight not shaped.

Crotch Curve - The Crotch Curve is shaped to fit between the legs. This seam cannot be seen when a person is standing in a normal erect position with the feet together. It must be shaped to the contour of the individual.

A lightweight wire coat hanger, which has been straightened out, may be placed between the legs and shaped to follow the contour of the body. Mark the front and back Waists on it and compare this shape to the shape of the pants pattern when they are laid out as in Figure 56 on page 38.

The Front Crotch Width determines how far in from the front of the body the Inseam will be. Normally 1 3/4" to 2" will place the Inseam in the correct position. However, if a woman has a pronounced tummy, this length may be extended 1" to 2" so that the pants will hang straight down the front (Figure 61).

The Back Crotch Width establishes how close fitting the pants will be at the buttocks. If this length is short, the Center Back seam will pull into the separation between the buttocks. If this length is too long, the pants will be baggy in the seat.

Front Inseam - The front Inseam must remain fairly straight. It may follow the leg taper established by the basic pattern and then flare out below the knee. But it must not flare out too much or there will be excess fullness between the legs.

Back Inseam - The back Inseam determines how close the pants will fit at the thigh. The more the back Inseam curves in, the closer the pants will fit. Figure 62 indicates the maximum amount that the patterns should curve in. If the pattern is closer than the alloted 3" of ease, there will be horizontal wrinkles under the buttocks.

BACK INSEAM

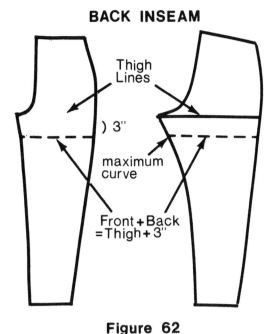

Figure 62

CROTCH CURVE

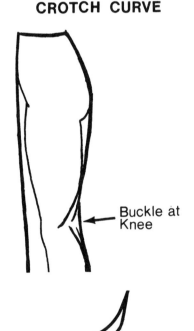

Figure 63

THE FITTING PROCEDURE

Step 1. If the skirt pattern has been previously fitted it may now be used to establish the darts and Side Seams. Match the front skirt pattern up with the front pants pattern at the Center Front and Waist. Transfer the dart and Side Seam shapes to the pants pattern. Repeat the procedure for the back pattern.

If the skirt pattern has not been previously fitted the darts and the Side Seams will be established in Step 5 below.

Step 2. Cut the patterns out of muslin. To fit the pants it is suggested that the seams be basted for the first fitting. Sew each leg separately. Turn one leg right side out and place it inside the other leg. Sew around the Center Back and the Crotch Curve. Leave the Center Front open for getting in and out of the pants.

Step 3. Put the pants on the person to be fitted with the seam allowances out. Adjust the pants from the side so that the pants legs hang straight down. The fabric should not break at the front or the back of the leg.

Step 4. Check the Crotch Curve for a comfortable fit. The Crotch Curve as it has been drafted will fit most people without any further adjustment. However, some people, particularly older women, may need to curve the back crotch lower. This keeps the pants from pivoting forward and buckling at the knee (Figure 63).

If the Crotch Curve must be adjusted, take the pants off and baste the curve lower. Trim the seam allowance down to 5/8" and try the pants on once again.

Step 5. After the pants have been adjusted to hang straight down the body the darts and the Side Seam must be adjusted to hold the pants accordingly. The same procedure used to fit the skirt may be used to fit the Waist to Hip region of the pants (pages 31 to 32).

Remember men will only have one dart. The dart for the buttock.

Step 6. Tie a string around the Waist. Adjust the pants so they hang straight down the body. Check them from the front, the side, and the back. The string at the Waist may be used to hold them in place.

THE WAIST

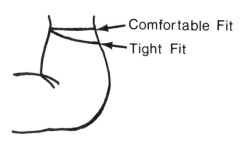

←Comfortable Fit

←Tight Fit

Figure 64

Step 7. The Side Seam may now be adjusted to establish how close fitting or loose the pants are going to be. The Waist will usually have about 1/2" of ease. The following chart lists the amount of ease at the Hips for fitted pants.

HIP EASE

	Tight	Snug	Comfortable
Women	1"	2"	3"
Men	1"	2"-3"	4"

Step 8. Have the person wearing the pants sit sideways on a chair and mark the Waist height at Center Back (Figure 64).

If the person wants the pants to look their best in a standing position the Waist at Center Back should be held as low as is comfortably possible while the person is sitting.

If the person is more interested in comfort of movement the Waist mark at Center Back should be at the natural waist line while the person is sitting.

Step 9. Have the person stand and mark the Waist just above the string using a felt tip marker. While marking the back make sure the string stays at the mark established in Step 8 above.

For Men - Measure down from this Waist to the desired top of the pants. This lower Waist should be used for the second fitting.

Step 10. Adjust the back Inseam, if desired, to make the pants tighter around the thigh.

Step 11. Take the pants off and continue with the general fitting procedures as described on page 30.

Styling Pants

Different styles of pants may be created by simply changing the shape of the Inseam, Side Seam and by altering the height of the Hem.

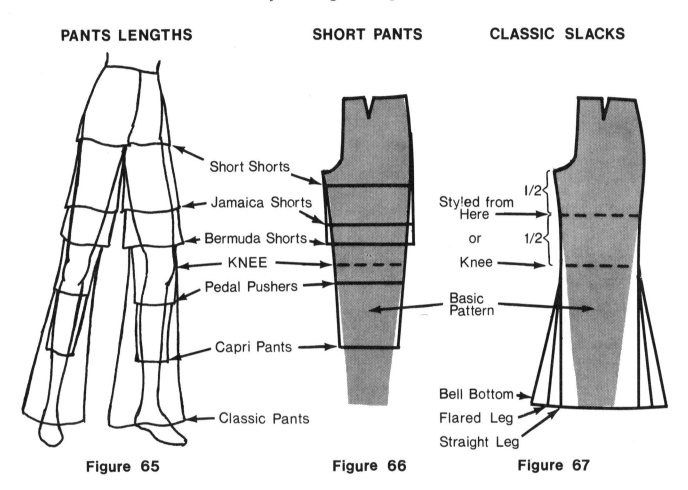

PANTS LENGTHS

Short Shorts
Jamaica Shorts
Bermuda Shorts
KNEE
Pedal Pushers
Capri Pants
Classic Pants

Figure 65

SHORT PANTS

Figure 66

CLASSIC SLACKS

Styled from Here   1/2
or   1/2
Knee
Basic Pattern
Bell Bottom
Flared Leg
Straight Leg

Figure 67

DETERMINING FULLNESS

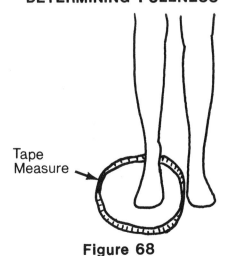

Tape Measure

Figure 68

The fullness desired in pants may be determined by placing a tape measure on the ground and shaping it in the size of the desired hem.

CULLOTTES

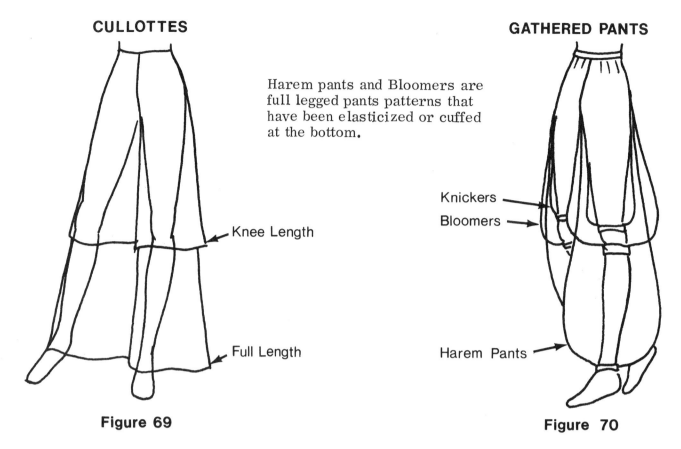

Harem pants and Bloomers are full legged pants patterns that have been elasticized or cuffed at the bottom.

Knee Length

Full Length

Figure 69

GATHERED PANTS

Knickers

Bloomers

Harem Pants

Figure 70

CROTCH WIDTH

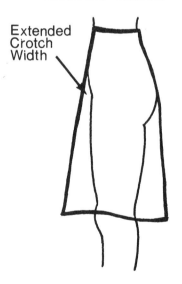

Extended Crotch Width

Draw string and elasticized waists may be created by making the Waist line larger than the Hip measurement and by not sewing in the darts. No zipper is required.

Culottes and Pant Dresses may be styled to hang out from the front of the body by extending the width of the Front Crotch Curve (usually 2").

Figure 71

FULL PANTS

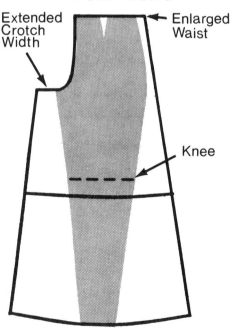

Extended Crotch Width

Enlarged Waist

Knee

Figure 72

For additional styling ideas procede to the sections describing waistbands, plackets, pockets, and cuffs.

THE BODICE PATTERN

The bodice pattern will be described as three separate patterns. First, the men's front pattern, then the back pattern for men and women, and finally the women's front pattern. The bodice is described in this manner so that the easiest patterns may be drafted first before progressing to the more involved patterns.

The body is divided between the front and the back by the Shoulder Seam (described on page 14) and by the Side Seam. The basic reference lines will be the Center Front or the Center Back line and the Waist line.

The Man's Body in Front

The man's body in front is a fairly simple form. The chest to waist area is straight up and down. The body curves at the shoulder and at the side (Figure 73).

The curves of the man's body in front bend in only one direction at a time. The curve from the chest up to the shoulder is higher than the curve from the front to the side. Fabric can bend in these two independent directions without being shaped by a dart or a seam.

This describes the standard shape of men's bodies, the shape that is used to design conventional men's clothes. Some men's bodies differ from this standard, such as barrel chested bodies. These variations of body styles present fitting and styling problems that will be discussed in the design section.

THE MAN'S SHAPE

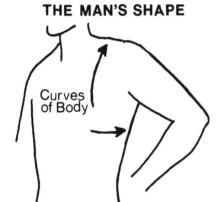

Curves of Body

Figure 73

THE PATTERN AND THE BODY

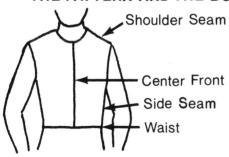

Shoulder Seam

Center Front

Side Seam

Waist

Figure 74

The Man's Front Pattern

One-half of the man's front will be used to draft the basic pattern. The Center Front and Waist will be established as the basic reference lines. The location of the Shoulder Seam and the Side Seam will be determined by measuring out from the basic reference lines. Then the neck curve and the armhole curve will be drawn in.

Measurements:

#20) Center Front to Waist _____

#2) Neck Width _____

#25) Side Front to Waist _____

#3) Shoulder Width _____

#27) Center Front/Waist
to Shoulder _____

#11) Waist _____

#4) Chest _____

#31) Armpit to Waist _____

BASIC REFERENCE LINES

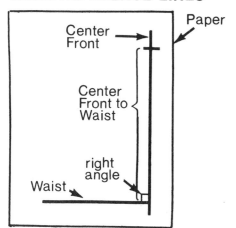

Figure 75

SHOULDER SEAM

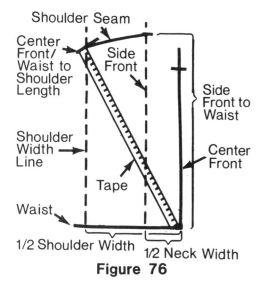

Figure 76

THE BASIC REFERENCE LINES

Step 1. On a sheet of paper approximately 24" by 24", draw a vertical line approximately 5" in from the right side of the paper (Figure 75). This is the Center Front line.

Step 2. About 5" from the bottom of the paper draw a line at right angles to the Center Front line. This is the Waist line.

Step 3. Mark off the Center Front to Waist measurement (#20) on the Center Front line.

THE SHOULDER SEAM

Step 4. On the Waist line measure out from the Center Front one-half the Neck Width measurement (#2) and make a mark. From this point draw a line that is parallel to the Center Front line (Figure 76). This is the Side Front line. Mark off the Side Front to Waist measurement (#25) on this line.

Step 5. On the Waist line measure out from the Center Front one-half the Shoulder Width measurement (#3) and make a mark. From this point draw a second line parallel to the Center Front line. This is the Shoulder Width line.

Step 6. To find the Shoulder Point, strike an arc from the Center Front at the Waist that is the Center Front/Waist to Shoulder length (#27). The Shoulder Point is located where this arc touches the Shoulder Width line.

To strike this arc, take a tape measure and find the Center Front/Waist to Shoulder length. Put one end of this length on the Center Front at the Waist and place the other end on the Shoulder Width line, holding the tape straight and taut.

Step 7. Draw a line from the top of the Side Front length (Step 4) to the Shoulder Point to form the Shoulder Seam.

THE SIDE SEAM

Step 8. On the Waist line mark off one-fourth of the Waist measurement (#11) measuring out from the Center Front. This is the Side Waist point.

One half of the Waist measurement would be the distance from the Center Front to the Center Back. To establish the location of the Side Seam this measurement may then be divided into half again (one-fourth of the total Waist measurement). The same thing will be done to the Chest measurement.

SIDE SEAM

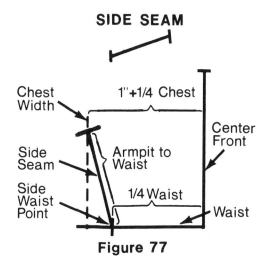

Figure 77

NECK CURVE

right angles

Figure 78

SEAM INTERSECTIONS

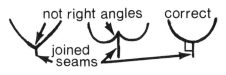

not right angles   correct

joined seams

Figure 79

ARMHOLE CURVE

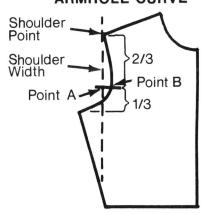

Figure 80

Step 9.   On the Waist line measure out from the Center Front line one inch plus one-fourth of the Chest measurement (#4) and make a mark. From this point draw a line parallel to the Center Front line (Figure 77). This is the Chest Width line.

One inch of ease is added to this measurement to compensate for the movement of the arms in relation to the body and for the movement of the chest.

Step 10.   Strike an arc from the Side Waist point using the Armpit to Waist measurement (#31) until it intersects the Chest Width line. Mark this point and draw a line connecting it to the Side Waist point. This line is the Side Seam.

THE NECK CURVE

Step 11.   The Neck curve is to be sketched in freehand (Figure 78). It is almost semi-circular in shape. The intersections of the Neck curve with the Center Front and the Shoulder Seam should be perpendicular. If this is not done, there will be an uneven shape where the separate patterns are joined together (Figure 79).

THE ARMHOLE CURVE

Step 12.   The Armhole curve is also sketched in freehand (Figure 80). Measure down from the Shoulder Point two-thirds of the distance from the Shoulder Point to the top of the Side Seam and mark point A on the Shoulder Width line. Measure three-quarters of an inch in from point A toward the Center Front line and mark point B.

The Armhole curve will be drawn straight from the Shoulder Point to point B. From here it will curve out to the top of the Side Seam.

The shape of the Neck curve and the Armhole curve are approximated in the drafting process. The exact shape will be determined by the contours of the individual body during the fitting.

SEAM ALLOWANCES

Add a 1 1/2" design and fitting seam allowance to the Side Seam and the Shoulder Seam. Add 1" fitting allowance to the Armhole and Neck curves and add 1" seam allowance to the Center Front for pinning the garment closed during the fitting. Add a 2" design and fitting allowance to the Waist.

The Shapes of the Back

Men's and women's backs have the same fundamental structure. There are two basic shapes of backs that may be found on either men or women. The first shape is the flat shouldered back and the other shape is the rounded shouldered back. To determine which shape you are working with look at the body from the side.

The flat shouldered back has the back of the arm even with the shoulder blades (Figure 81). Place a yardstick across the shoulder blades so that it is parallel to the floor. Notice that both the back of the arms and the shoulder blades touch the yardstick. The fabric covering this shape of back may bend from the Shoulder Seam down the back without being shaped by a dart.

Round shouldered backs have arms that pitch forward from the shoulder blades (Figure 82). If a round shouldered person were to back up flat against a wall, the back of their arms would not touch the wall, only their shoulder blades. Rounded shoulders require a dart or seam to shape the fabric because it must bend in two directions at one time (Figure 83). It must bend in a vertical direction from the Shoulder Seam down the back. And it must bend in a horizontal direction from the Center Back around to the to the Armhole seam.

Both the flat shouldered back and the round shouldered back must have a dart in the area from the bottom of the shoulder blades to the waist. All bodies bend in two directions in this area. They bend horizontally from Center Back to the Side Seam and vertically from the bottom of the shoulders in to the Waist (Figure 84).

The Back Pattern

The back pattern will be drafted for the flat shouldered back first. An adjustment can then be made to allow for round shouldered backs during the fitting.

The back pattern will be drafted in almost the same way as the man's front pattern. The main difference is made by adding an extra allowance for the back darts.

FLAT SHOULDERS

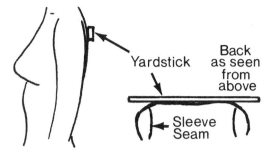

Figure 81

ROUNDED SHOULDERS

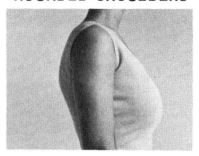

Figure 82

UPPER BACK SHAPE

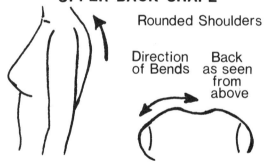

Figure 83

LOWER BACK SHAPE

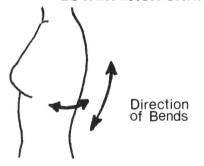

Figure 84

Measurements:

#28) Center Back _____

#2) Neck Width _____

#29) Side Back _____

#3) Shoulder Width _____

#30) Center Back/Waist
to Shoulder _____

#11) Waist _____

#4) Chest _____ (or)

#8) Back Bust _____

#31) Armpit to Waist _____

BASIC REFERENCE LINES

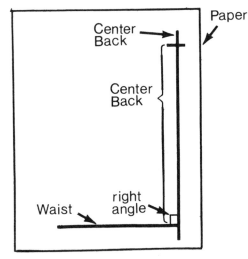

Figure 85

SHOULDER SEAM

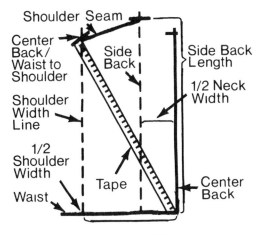

Figure 86

THE BASIC REFERENCE LINES

Step 1. On a sheet of paper draw a vertical line 5" in from the right hand side of the paper (Figure 85). This is the Center Back line.

Step 2. About 5" up from the bottom of the paper draw a line at right angles to the Center Back line. This is the Waist line.

Step 3. Mark off the Center Back measurement (#28) on the Center Back line measuring up from the Waist line.

THE SHOULDER SEAM

Step 4. On the Waist line measure out from the Center Back line one-half of the Neck measurement (#2) and make a mark. From this point draw a line parallel to the Center Back line (Figure 86). This is the Side Back line. Mark off the Side Back measurement (#29) on this line.

Step 5. On the waist line measure out from the Center Back line one-half of the Shoulder Width measurement (#3) and make a mark. From this point draw a line parallel to the Center Back line. This is the Shoulder Width line.

Step 6. To find the Shoulder Point, strike an arc from the Center Back at the Waist that is the Center Back/Waist to Shoulder length (#30). The Shoulder Point is located where this arc touches the Shoulder Width line.

Step 7. Draw a line from the top of the Side Back length (Step 4) to the Shoulder Point to form the Shoulder Seam.

49

SIDE SEAM

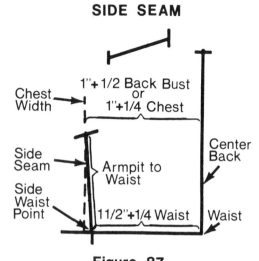

Figure 87

NECK CURVE

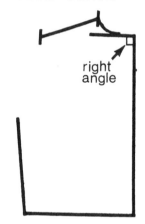

Figure 88

ARMHOLE CURVE

Figure 89

THE SIDE SEAM

Step 8. On the Waist line mark off one and one-half inch plus one-fourth of the Waist measurement (#11) measuring out from the Center Back. This is the Side Waist point (Figure 87).

The one and one-half inch added to the Waist measurement is a dart allowance for the back dart. The back dart will be fitted according to the contours of the individual body rather than drafted in at this point.

Step 9. For Men – On the Waist line measure out from the Center Back line one inch plus one-fourth the Chest measurement (#4) and make a mark. From this point draw a line parallel to the Center Back line. This is the Chest Width line.

For Women – On the Waist line measure out from the Center Back line one inch plus one-half the Back Bust measurement (#8) and make a mark. From this point draw a line parallel to the Center Back line. This is the Chest Width line.

Step 10. Strike an arc from the Side Waist point using the Armpit to Waist measurement (#31) until it intersects the Chest Width line. Mark this point and draw a line connecting it to the Side Waist point. This is the Side Seam.

THE NECK CURVE

Step 11. At the top of the Center Back length draw a line at right angles to the Center Back line. Extend this line to the Side Back line (Figure 88). Draw in a short curve from the Shoulder Seam to this line. This is the Neck Curve.

The neck across the back is fairly flat. The back Neck Curve will, therefore, not dip down as much as the front Neck Curve.

THE ARMHOLE CURVE

Step 12. The back Armhole Curve is very shallow. It starts out at right angles to the Shoulder Seam and curves slightly until it meets the Side Seam line (Figure 89).

SEAM ALLOWANCES

Add a 1 1/2" design and fitting seam allowance to the Side Seam and the Shoulder Seam. Add a 1" fitting allowance to the Armhole and Neck curves and add a 2" design and fitting allowance at the Waist. The Center Back line will be a fold line.

The Woman's Body in Front

SHAPE OF BUST

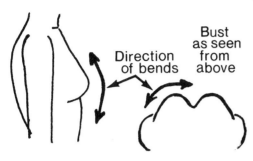

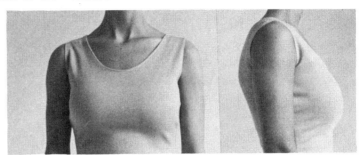

Figure 90

THE TWO BUST SHAPES

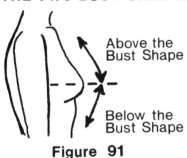

Figure 91

THE BUST AND THE DART

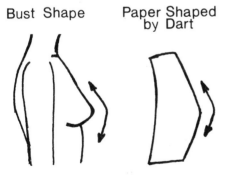

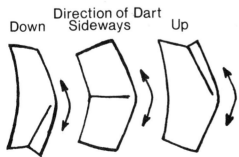

Figure 92

Women's bodices vary in the front according to the size and shape of the bust. The exact shape of the bust is very important in determining how the finished garments will hang.

The bust is shaped in two directions at the same time. The horizontal direction bends from the Center Front around to the Side Seam (Figure 90). The vertical direction slopes down from the shoulder to the apex of the bust and then bends into the Waist. These two simultaneous curves of the bust make a dart in fabric mandatory if the garment is to fit properly.

The vertical curve should also be divided into two parts (Figure 91). The first part will be for the shape of the bust from the Shoulder Seam to the bust. This will be referred to as the Above the Bust shape. The second part is the shape from the bust to the Waist. This area will be referred to as the Below the Bust shape.

It is necessary to make this two part distinction because while most garments must fit the Above the Bust area, not every garment will be close fitting Below the Bust. Each of these two shapes also affects the grain lines of garments differently.

Important Note - While these two shapes will be referred to separately from this point onward, it is important to remember that they are two shapes for the single contour of the bust. A single dart may therefore be used to make fabric fit both shapes. And this dart may come from any seam as long as the dart points to the bust.

To understand this concept better, take the piece of paper used to create the dart in the Introduction (page 10). Hold it in a vertical position so that it reflects the shape of the bust (Figure 92). Now turn it around so that the dart points down, sideways, and finally turn it up. Notice the shape does not change.

THE PATTERN AND THE BODY

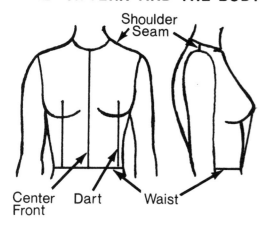

Figure 93

Measurements:

#20) Center Front to Waist _____

#2) Neck Width _____

#25) Side Front to Waist _____

#24) Side Front to Bust _____

#9) Bust to Bust _____

#3) Shoulder Width _____

#26) Bust to Shoulder _____

#5) Upper Chest _____

#6) Full Bust _____

#7) Front Bust _____

#8) Back Bust _____

#31) Armpit to Waist _____

#11) Waist _____

BASIC REFERENCE LINES

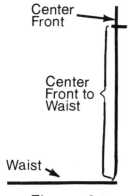

Figure 94

The Woman's Front Pattern

The woman's front pattern will be drafted for one-half of the front. The Center Front and the Waist will be the basic reference lines. The apex of the bust will also be established as an important reference point.

Unlike the other basic patterns, the dart for the bust may be included in the drafting process because the apex of the bust may be easily located with measurements. The bust dart for the basic pattern is drafted in at the Waist line because this is the best location of the dart for both fitting purposes and for pattern alteration purposes. Other dart locations will be given in the section on pattern alterations.

THE BASIC REFERENCE LINES

Step 1. Draw a vertical line on the right side of the paper that is the Center Front to Waist length (#20). This is the Center Front line (Figure 94).

Step 2. At the bottom of this length draw a line at right angles to the Center Front line. This is the Waist line.

THE BUST POINT

Step 3. On the Waist line measure out from the Center Front line one-half the Neck Width measurement (#2) and make a mark. From this point draw a line that is parallel to the Center Front line (Figure 95). This is the Side Front line. Measure up from the Waist and mark off the Side Front to Waist length (#25).

Step 4. Measure down from the top of the Side Front length the Side Front to Bust measurement (#24). Draw a short line at right angles to the Side Front line at this point. This establishes the height of the bust.

Step 5. On the Waist line measure out from the Center Front line one-half the Bust to Bust measurement (#9) and make a mark. From this point draw a line parallel to the Center Front line. This is the Bust Width line. The Bust Point is located where this line crosses the line established in Step 4.

BUST POINT

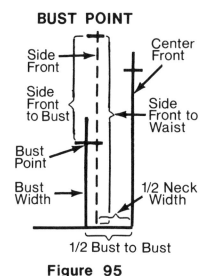

Figure 95

SHOULDER SEAM

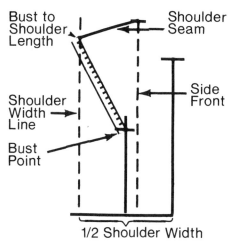

Figure 96

THE SHOULDER SEAM

Step 6. On the Waist line measure out from the Center Front line one-half the Shoulder Width measurement (#3) and make a mark. From this point draw a line that is parallel to the Center Front line (Figure 96). This is the Shoulder Width line.

Step 7. To find the Shoulder Point strike an arc from the Bust Point that is the Bust to Shoulder length (#26). The Shoulder Point is located where this arc touches the Shoulder Width line.

Step 8. Draw a line from the Shoulder Point to the top of the Side Front length. This is the Shoulder Seam.

THE BUST DART

The dart width for the Above the Bust shape will now be drafted in. This dart width will be referred to as the "A" Dart Width ("A" for above). This "A" dart will affect the way the side of the front pattern is drafted as will be seen. The size of the dart must, therefore, be determined by the size of the bust.

Step 9. To determine the size of the "A" Dart Width subtract the Upper Chest measurement (#5) from the Full Bust measurement (#6). The difference between these two measurements may be used to find the size of the dart from the "A" Dart Width Chart.

Upper Chest (#5)		Full Bust (#6)		See Chart
	minus		equals	
_____		_____		_____

"A" DART WIDTH CHART

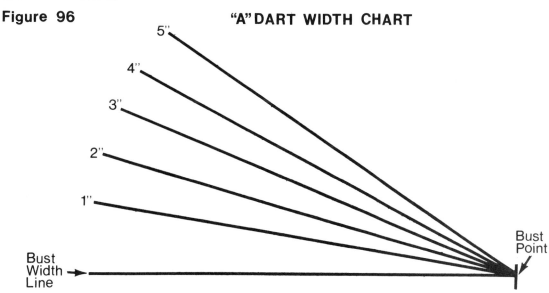

THE DART

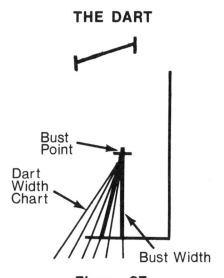

Figure 97

RAISED WAIST

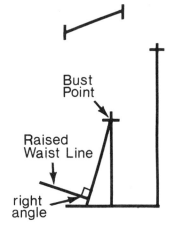

Figure 98

Step 10. Place the "A" Dart Width Chart under the pattern and line up the Bust Width line and the Bust point of the chart with the Bust Width line and the Bust point of the pattern (Figure 97). Trace the correct dart width from the chart. This line will be the outside leg of the "A" dart.

This chart may be used for both full sized patterns and quarter scale patterns because it is the angle of the dart that determines the dart width.

THE RAISED WAIST LINE

Step 11. Measure the distance from the Bust point to the Waist and mark this length on the outside leg of the "A" dart. From this point draw a line at right angles to the outside leg of the dart. This is the Raised Waist line (Figure 98).

The preceding steps have been designed to place the correct dart width for the Above the Bust contour of the body on the pattern below the Bust point.

To better visualize this concept, notice what happens when the pattern is cut through its full length starting at the Bust Width line and the dart is taped closed (Figure 99). The dart angle now appears above the bust. The Center Front and the Waist line are positioned exactly as they were for drafting both the man's front pattern and the back pattern.

EFFECT OF DART AND RAISED WAIST

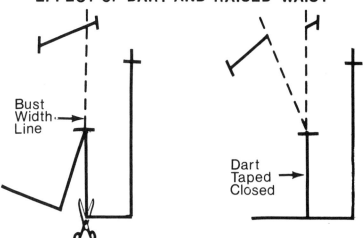

Figure 99

54

CHEST WIDTH

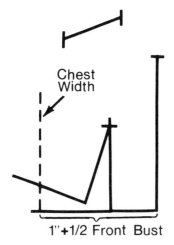

Figure 100

1"+1/2 Front Bust

SIDE SEAM

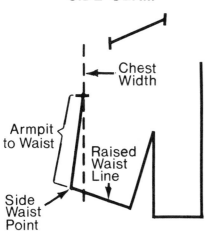

Figure 101

THE SIDE SEAM

Step 12. On the Waist line measure out from the Center Front one inch plus one-half the Front Bust measurement (#7) and make a mark. From this point draw a line that is parallel to the Center Front line (Figure 100). This is the Chest Width line. The one inch is the basic fitting ease.

As was mentioned in the section on measurements, it is difficult to accurately determine the best location for the Side Seam. This location will divide the Full Bust into a Front Bust and a Back Bust measurement. The chart below gives the approximate differences between the front measurement and the back measurement according to bust size. The bust size is determined by subtracting the Upper Chest measurement from the Full Bust measurement

APPROXIMATE BUST SIZE

Full Bust (#6)	minus	Upper Chest (#5)	equals	
_____		_____		_____

Front Bust (#7)	minus	Back Bust (#8)	equals	
_____		_____		_____

	1"	2"	3"	4"	5"
Full Bust – Upper Chest	1"	2"	3"	4"	5"
Front Bust – Back Bust	0"	1"	2"	3"	4"

This chart may be used to double check your measurement chart. Severe differences should be carefully rechecked by retaking the measurements. The exact location of the Side Seam will be established during the fitting.

Step 13. To determine the length of the raised portion of the Waist line subtract one-half of the Bust to Bust measurement (#9) from one-half of the Front Bust measurement (#7). Mark this length on the Raised Waist line measuring out from the outside leg of the dart (Figure 101). This mark is the Side Waist point.

1/2 Front Bust (#7)	minus	1/2 Bust to Bust (#9)	equals	
_____		_____		_____

Step 14. Strike an arc from the Side Waist point using the Armpit to Waist measurement (#31) until it intersects the Chest Width line. Mark this point and draw a line connecting it to the Side Waist point. This is the Side Seam.

BELOW THE BUST DART

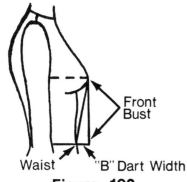

Figure 102

DART WIDTHS

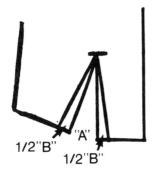

Figure 103

NECK CURVE

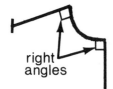

Figure 104

ARMHOLE CURVE

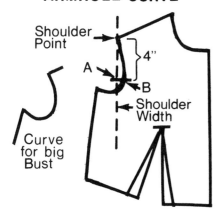

Figure 105

THE "B" DART WIDTH

The Front Bust measurement was used to determine the width of the pattern at the Waist line (Step 13). The difference between the Front Bust measurement and the Waist measurement is the allowance required to create the dart for the Below the Bust shape, the "B" dart width (Figure 102).

Step 15. Subtract one-fourth of the Waist measurement (#11) from one-half the Front Bust measurement (#7). The difference is the "B" Dart Width.

1/2 Front Bust (#7)	1/4 Waist	"B" Dart Width
	minus	equals
_____	_____	_____

Step 16. Mark off one-half of the "B" Dart Width on either side of the "A" dart(Figure 103). Draw lines from these marks to the Bust Point.

THE NECK CURVE

Step 17. The Neck Curve will be drawn in freehand (Figure 104). It is almost semi-circular in shape. Be sure the intersections of the Neck Curve with the Center Front and the Shoulder Seam are at right angles.

THE ARMHOLE CURVE

Step 18. The Armhole Curve is also sketched in freehand. Measure down from the Shoulder Point on the Shoulder Width line 3 1/2" to 4" and mark point A (Figure 105). Measure three-quarters of an inch in from point A towards the Center Front line and mark point B.

Step 19. Draw the Armhole Curve from the Shoulder Point to point B. Then curve it out to the top of the Side Seam. Big busts will require a more pronounced curve.

SEAM ALLOWANCES

Add a 1 1/2" design and fitting allowance to the Side Seam and Shoulder Seam. Add a 1" fitting allowance to the Armhole and Neck curves and 1" to the Center Front for pinning the garment closed during the fitting. Add a 2" design and fitting allowance to the Waist.

FITTING THE SHOULDERS

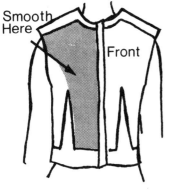

Figure 106

SHOULDER SEAM

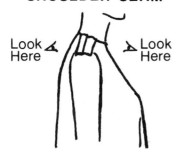

Figure 107

THE FRONT DART

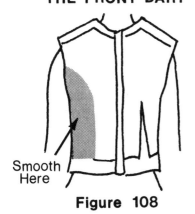

Figure 108

Fitting the Bodice

The fitted bodice will be the basis for coats, shirts, blouses, and dresses. An accurate fit at this point will save a great deal of time later when these garments are drafted.

Start by first fitting one-half of the body with a pinning. After this fitting, the muslin may be basted together for a second fitting. Adjustments for asymmetrical bodies will be made during this second fitting.

Step 1. Transfer the Center Front and Center Back lines, the seam lines and the seam allowance lines, and the woman's front dart from the paper patterns to the muslin.

Step 2. Cut out the muslin and pin the front Shoulder Seams to the back Shoulder Seams but do not pin the Side Seams.

Step 3. Put the muslin on the person to be fitted and pin the Center Front closed.

Step 4. Adjust the Shoulder Seam, if necessary, so that the Center Front and Center Back lines on the muslin follow the Center Front and Center Back of the body. The fabric should fit smoothly on the front and back of the body as is illustrated in Figure 106.

The Shoulder Seam for this basic bodice should be on the top of the shoulder. Check for the correct placement by looking straight at this seam from the front and then from the back (Figure 107). Looking from the front, you should not be able to see the fabric of the back pattern. Looking from the back, you should not be able to see the fabric of the front pattern. Adjust the seam as necessary to achieve this.

Pin the Shoulder Seams carefully because garments for the upper body hang from the shoulders. If the correct slope of the shoulders is not established, then the fabric will not hang smoothly.

Step 5. For Women - Fit in the front dart by holding the fabric flat in front and smoothing down the side of the body as is illustrated in Figure 108. Pin out the excess fabric at the Waist to form the Dart Width.

HOLLOW ABOVE BUST

Figure 109

DART POINT

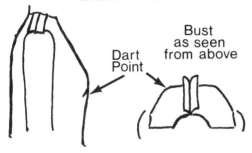

Figure 110

DART FOLDS

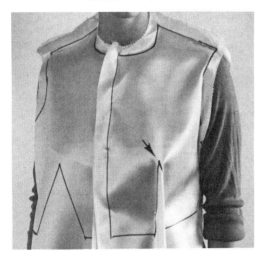

Figure 111

TOP OF DART

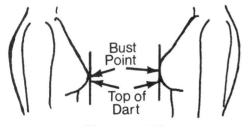

Figure 112

Women with a hollow between the bust and the Shoulder Seam (Figure 109) will not be able to smooth out this area completely. This hollow can only be fitted by placing a dart or seam between the armhole and the apex of the bust. See the section on styling the Princess Seam for further information on this matter.

Step 5 & 6. For Men - There will be no front dart for men. The only adjustments required in the front will be at the Shoulder Seam (Step 4) and at the Side Seam (Step 8).

Step 6. For Women - After the appropriate Dart Width has been established, the top of the dart must be determined. There are two ways of doing this. The first way is to look at the body and determine where the curves start (Figure 110) as was done for fitting the skirt.

The second way of determining the top of the dart is to look at the fabric (Figure 111). The folds of the fabric naturally point to the best location for the top of the dart. It is easiest to see these folds in the fabric if the person being fitted stands in a strong directional light. Stand near a window to catch either the early morning or late afternoon sun.

Both techniques for determining the top of the dart should be used to establish an accurate fitting. The point of the dart should be marked by placing a pin horizontally through the fabric so that it catches only one or two threads.

Important note - You will notice that the top of the fitted dart is not right at the Bust Point. The dart should stop short of the flat part of the front of the bust (Figure 112). The more the bust is rounded in the front, the further away the top of the dart will be from the Bust Point. A circle may be drawn around the Bust Point indicating the flat part of the front of the bust. All darts should stop short of this circle. The chart below gives the approximate dimension of the radius of this circle for various bust sizes (Full Bust measurement minus Upper Chest measurement).

BUST CIRCLE

Full Bust – Upper Chest	1"	2"	3"	4"
Radius of Bust Circle	1"	$1\frac{1}{2}$"	2"	$2\frac{1}{2}$"

Step 7. The next step is to establish the back dart. Two different fitting procedures will be described. One fitting procedure will be for flat or slightly rounded backs and the other will be for pronounced rounded backs.

LOWER BACK DART

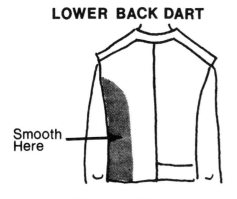

Smooth Here

Figure 113

LOWER BACK - DART POINT

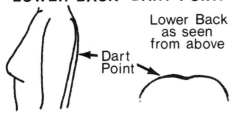

Lower Back as seen from above

Dart Point

Figure 114

UPPER BACK DART

Excess Fabric

Figure 115

UPPER BACK - DART POINT

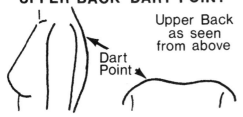

Upper Back as seen from above

Dart Point

Figure 116

SHOULDER BLADES

Upper Dart Point

Lower Dart Point

Figure 117

Flat Backs - Hold the center of the back flat and shape the side so that it fits smoothly (Figure 113). Pin out the dart width at the Waist. Mark the top of the dart by looking at the folds of the fabric. Then check this location by looking at the side of the body and then down at the top of the back (Figure 114).

Rounded Backs - Slightly rounded backs may be fitted by the above technique. Severely rounded backs will require such a large lower dart that there will not be enough fabric left at the side for a Side Seam. If this is the case, use the following technique to establish two darts for the back.

Mark the horizontal grain of the fabric across the middle of the shoulder blades. This grain line may be marked either with a felt tip pen or by pulling out a single horizontal thread from the fabric. Keep this line parallel to the ground and shape in the lower back dart as described above.

You will notice there is now extra fabric at the armhole (Figure 115). This fabric will be shaped into a dart. Find the point of this dart by determining where the body bends around to the side and where the body bends up to the shoulder (Figure 116). Then smooth out the excess fabric at the armhole and pin it into a dart.

The point of the upper dart will be about one inch further out from the Center Back than the point of the lower dart. This is due to the shape of the shoulder blades in back (Figure 117).

The upper dart is fitted into the muslin as a horizontal dart. Later, after the second fitting, this dart will be changed into a vertical dart coming from the Shoulder seam.

Step 8. The Side Seam may now be fitted by smoothing the fabric from the back into the fabric from the front. It will be more accurate at this point to pin out the normal ease left for the chest. This ease may be added back in before the second fitting.

Be careful during this step not to pull the Center Front and the Center Back out of alignment. It may be helpful to roughly pin out the Side Seam on the side not being fitted just to help hold the Center Front and Center Back in place.

Step 9. Mark the Neck Curve with a felt tip pen. You may wish to review the correct placement for the Neck Curve as it was described on page 14. Make sure that the point where the front Neck Curve touches the Shoulder Seam is the same point where the back Neck Curve touches the Shoulder Seam.

THE SHAPE OF THE ARMHOLE

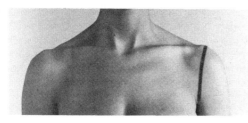 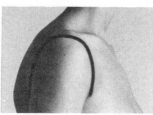 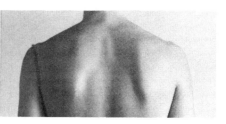

Figure 118

ARMHOLE CURVE

Fabric
Buckling

Figure 119

Step 10. The Armhole Curve may be drawn in next. Figure 118 shows how this curve should follow the body. Establish the Shoulder Point first (see page 14). Then mark where the fabric buckles between the arm and the body (Figure 119). Blend from this mark to the Shoulder Point. Continue the curve under the arm. Repeat this procedure for the back.

Step 11. Place a string around the Waist. Make sure that it is parallel to the floor around the entire body. With a felt tip pen mark the location of the string on the muslin.

Note for Women – The Waist line on women may be anywhere between the top of the pelvic bone and the bottom of the rib cage. This distance is between two and three inches. The Waist has been determined, up to this point, by placing a string around the body and tying it snugly. The string will have a tendency to find a level half way between the pelvic bone and the rib cage. Some women may prefer a lower Waist on their finished garments, just above the pelvic bone for example. The Waist may be adjusted to the desired height by placing the string at that level and marking the muslin.

The fitted skirt should be put on to make sure that the Waist established for the skirt is at the same height as the Waist for the bodice.

Step 12. The bodice may now be removed. Mark all of the pin locations carefully. Make sure the pin locations for the Shoulder and the Side Seams are marked on both the front and the back patterns.

Place one pin through the muslin at right angles to the Side Seam and another pin at right angles to the Shoulder Seam. Mark the front and back patterns at these two pins. These marks will be used to line up the seams when they are sewn. Remove the pins.

DART LOCATION

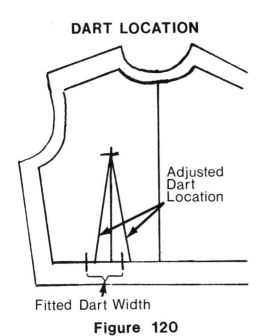

Fitted Dart Width

Figure 120

SIDE SEAM LOCATION

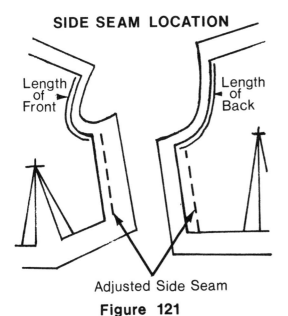

Adjusted Side Seam

Figure 121

Step 13. The lower dart should be adjusted as follows to achieve the best appearance. Find the top of the dart and from this point draw a line parallel to the Center Back line (Figure 120). This line will be the Center Fold of the dart. On the Waist line, find the marks indicating the Dart Width and measure this distance. Mark off half the Dart Width on either side of the Center Fold. Connect these marks to the top of the dart with straight lines.

The upper dart for rounded backs will be left as is for now.

Step 14. To adjust the Side Seam to the proper location, measure the length of the front Armhole Curve and the length of the back Armhole Curve. If these two measurements are not exactly the same length, adjust the Side Seams forward or backwards until they are the same length (Figure 121). This step places the Side Seam in the middle of the arm.

Add the ease back in at the top of the Side Seam. The distance from the Center Front to the Side Seam to the Center Back should be equal to two inches plus one-half the Chest measurement for men or two inches plus one-half of the Full Bust measurement for women.

Procede with the general fitting procedures as described on page 30, but read "The Fabric Grain and the Waist" (page 62) before you make the final corrections to the paper patterns.

LOWER "A" DART

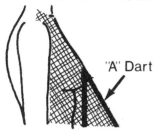

"A" Dart

Figure 122

UPPER "A" DART

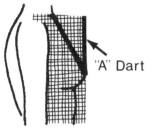

"A" Dart

Figure 123

FABRIC GRAIN

Figure 124

BUST SIZE

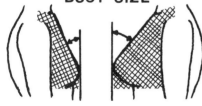

Figure 125

"B" DART

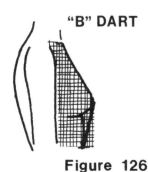

Figure 126

Fabric Grain and the Waist

Darts, when they are shaped to fit the contours of the body, change the direction of the grain of the fabric. This fact is an important design consideration, particularly for garments that are to fit the upper body. It is important, therefore, to understand how to control the grain by varying the size and location of the darts.

THE BUST DART

The bust dart shapes fabric for two areas of the body. The Above the Bust area is shaped by the "A" Dart Width and the Below the Bust area is shaped by the "B" Dart Width (page 51).

The "A" Dart Width when it is placed below the bust allows the fabric to hang straight down from the bust. This may be seen in the Fitted Bodice pattern. In this location, however, the grain at the side of the bust is not parallel to the floor (Figure 122). When the "A" Dart Width is placed above the bust, the fabric will hang straight down from the bust and the horizontal grain of the fabric will be parallel to the floor (Figure 123). For garments that are to hang freely from the bust, the horizontal grain of the fabric must be parallel to the floor to insure a good fit (Figure 124).

The exact size of the "A" Dart Width directly depends on the size of the bust and the resulting slope from the shoulder to the bust (Figure 125).

Notice that the size of the "B" Dart Width may be changed without affecting the direction of the grain of the fabric on the side of the body (Figure 126).

To translate this concept into usable terms, the exact size of the "A" Dart Width must be determined from the fitting.

Step 1. After all of the corrections from the second fitting have been clearly indicated, remove the basting.

Step 2. Starting at the Bust Point, draw a line parallel to the Center Front line. This is the Bust Width line. Cut the muslin along this line from the Waist to the Shoulder Seam (Figure 127). This creates a front section and a side section for the pattern.

CUTTING THE FRONT

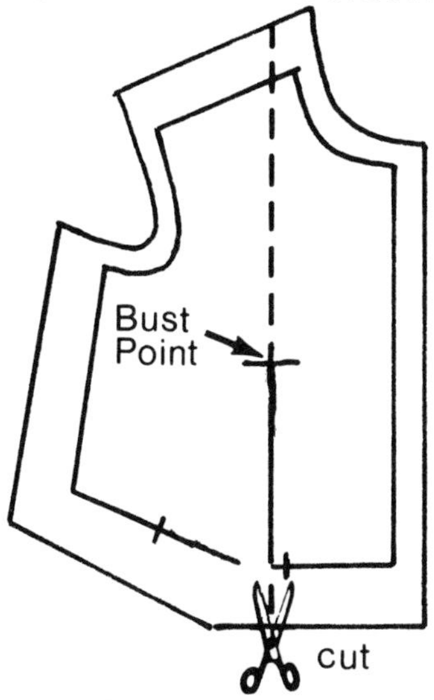

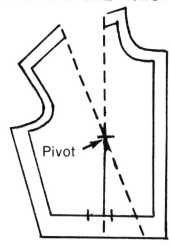

Figure 127

ALIGNING THE WAIST

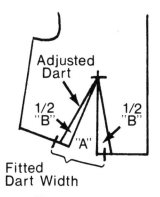

Figure 128

CORRECTED DART

Figure 129

Step 3. Place these two sections together at the Bust Point and pivot them until both Waist lines are at right angles to the Center Front line (Figure 128). Mark the location of the Bust Width line from the front section on to the side section from the Waist to the Bust Point. This line is the outside leg of the "A" Dart.

Step 4. Place the front and side sections back together again along the cutting line. Subtract the "A" Dart Width from the total pinned out Dart Width from the fitting. The remaining Dart Width is the "B" Dart Width. Mark off half of the "B" Dart Width on either side of the "A" Dart Width (Figure 129). Connect these marks to the Bust Point.

Important Note – The markings for the bust dart on the basic pattern are all shaped to the Bust Point. The basic pattern must be set up this way for the pattern alterations and design techniques that are to follow. Darts in the finished garments will always stop short of the Bust Circle.

ROUNDED BACKS

Rounded backs will have the same effect on the fabric of the back as the bust has on the fabric of the front. Figure 130 shows how the fabric on the side of the back will be off grain unless there is a dart in the Shoulder Seam. Notice also that the lower back dart can be taken in and let out without affecting the grain at all.

Figure 131 shows how the back pattern for a rounded back is similar to the woman's front pattern. Notice the rise at the side of the Waist. A flat back will not have this rise.

BACK FABRIC GRAIN

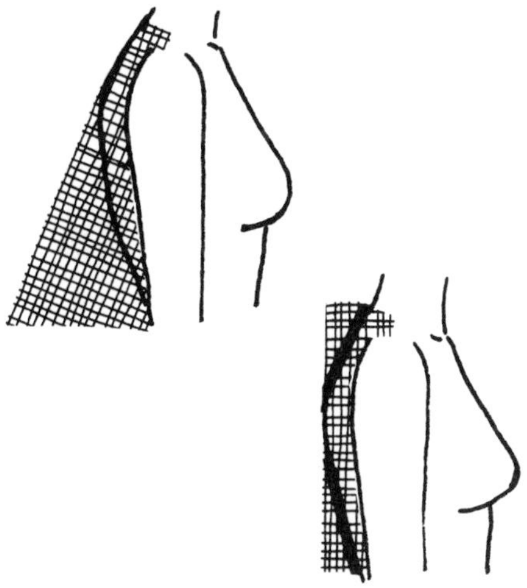

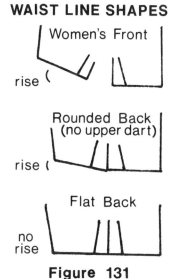

Figure 130

WAIST LINE SHAPES

Women's Front

rise

Rounded Back
(no upper dart)

rise

Flat Back

no
rise

Figure 131

UPPER DART LOCATION

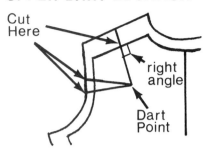

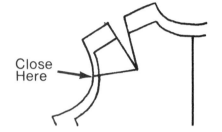

Figure 132

CUTTING THE BACK

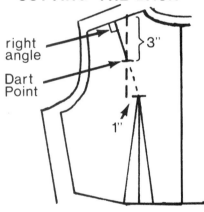

Figure 133

ALIGNING THE BACK

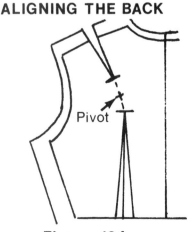

Figure 134

The following procedures may be used to adjust the back pattern. The upper dart will be adjusted to the correct size to keep the grain of the fabric parallel to the floor.

Muslins with Two Darts

The fitting for this muslin was done so that the grain across the back would be kept parallel to the floor. It will only be necessary to change the dart from the armhole to the Shoulder Seam.

Step 1. Draw a line at right angles to the Shoulder Seam so that it intersects with the point of the upper dart (Figure 132). Cut along this line.

Step 2. Cut out the wedge of the dart shaped into the armhole and put these two edges together. The resulting shape is the size of the upper back dart.

Muslins with One Dart

Part of the lower dart must be transfered to a shoulder dart so that the entire Waist is at right angles to Center Back.

Step 1. Measure the distance from the Center Back to the Center Fold of the lower dart. Add one inch to this length and draw a line parallel to Center Back from this point (Figure 133).

Step 2. On this line, measure down three inches from the Shoulder Seam and make a mark. This is the point of the upper dart.

Step 3. Draw a line at right angles to the Shoulder Seam so that it intersects with the point of the upper dart.

Step 4. Cut through the muslin along the Center Fold of the lower dart. Curve over to the point of the upper dart and cut through the line established in Step 3.

Step 5. Pivot out the lower dart until the entire Waist line is at right angles to the Center Back line. Pivot the patterns at a point half way between the two dart points. The upper Dart Width is the distance between the two cut lines of the Shoulder Seam (Figure 134). Anchor the muslin in place as it is laying now and trace the corrections onto paper.

Transfer the corrected markings from both the front and the back patterns back onto paper for a permanent record.

FITTING YOURSELF

MIRROR LOCATIONS

Mirrors as seen from above

|◄ 3 feet ►|

✕ ← Stand
Here

Figure 135

Fitting yourself, according to some authorities, should never be attempted. However, it you do not have someone who has the time and the ability to help you with a fitting, you will be better off to take the time and fit yourself.

Once you have done this initial fitting, you can use the basic patterns to create other garments that will require little if any fitting. It would also be a good idea to make the custom dress form described later in the book. This will save you a great deal of time and effort in your sewing.

The problem with fitting yourself is that you must not twist or turn your body in the least. Your upper arms must also be kept at the side of your body. Inappropriate movement of the body will make an accurate fitting impossible.

Fitting yourself will require a set up using two mirrors (Figure 135). One mirror should preferably be a full length wall mirror. The other should be a moveable wall mirror that can be placed on an artist easel or secured to an ironing board that is standing on end. The mirrors must be positioned so that you can clearly see your back without twisting.

A typewriter ribbon will also be required to mark the back where you would not otherwise be able to reach.

Fitting yourself requires that you take the muslin on and off a number of times. Each time the Center Front must be carefully secured in the same position. It is a good idea, therefore, to put a zipper, snaps, or velcro down the Center Front.

Fitting the Bodice on Yourself

Step 1. Transfer the markings from the paper pattern to the muslin and cut it out.

Step 2. Pin the Shoulder Seams together and put the muslin on. Check to see that the Center Front and Center Back of the muslin line up with the body and that the fabric fits smoothly on this part of the body (see page 57).

If the measurements were taken correctly, there should be only minor adjustments to the Shoulder Seams. If a major adjustment is necessary, correct it as follows.

DART HEIGHT

Figure 136

SHOULDER BLADE WIDTH

Figure 137

Step 2a. Unpin one Shoulder Seam. On a close fitting undergarment, such as a tee shirt or body suit, indicate the correct Shoulder Seam placement with pins. Place one pin close to the neck, one at the Shoulder Point, and place one pin at right angles to the Shoulder Seam.

Step 2b. Place yourself so that you can look into the mirrors and see your back clearly without twisting. Keep your upper arms close to your body and adjust the Shoulder Seam with the hand that is opposite the side being fitted. Once the fabric has been correctly adjusted, pin the seam allowance of the Shoulder Seam to the fitted undergarment.

Step 2c. With a felt tip pen mark the locations of the three pins which indicate the Shoulder Seam placement. The one pin at right angles to the Shoulder Seam will be used to line up the front seam with the back seam.

Step 2d. Repeat the entire procedure for the front pattern.

Step 3. After the corrections have been made to the Shoulder Seams, transfer the marks from the fitted side to the unfitted side. Baste the seams together. Put the muslin on and recheck the fit.

Step 4. For Women - Follow the regular fitting procedure to establish the front dart. You will have to look at the side of the body in the mirror to determine the correct height of the dart.
Remove the muslin. Transfer the fitting marks from the fitted side to the unfitted side and baste in the darts. Put the muslin back on and recheck the fit.

Step 5. The back dart must be fitted next. To determine the point of the dart, look at the side of your body in the mirror. Take the typewriter ribbon and put it around the shoulders at the height where the back starts to curve into the Waist (Figure 136). Move the typewriter ribbon back and forth slightly to leave a line on the muslin.

Step 6. Take the muslin off. Measure the distance from the inside of one shoulder blade to the inside of the other shoulder blade (Figure 137).

DART FOLD

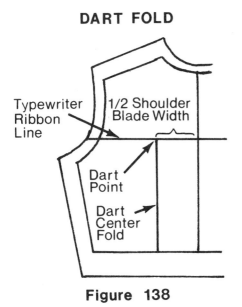

Typewriter Ribbon Line

1/2 Shoulder Blade Width

Dart Point

Dart Center Fold

Figure 138

CUTTING THE FOLD

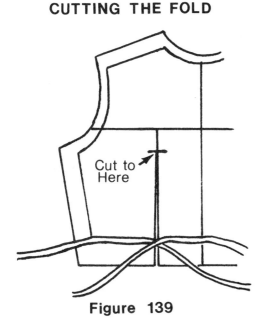

Cut to Here

Figure 139

SHAPING THE BACK

Fit Here

Figure 140

Step 7. Divide the distance between the shoulder blades in half. Mark this length on the Waist line measuring out from Center Back. Draw a line parallel to the Center Back line from this point (Figure 138). This is the Center Fold of the dart.

The point of the dart is located where the Center Fold crosses the line made by the typewriter ribbon.

Step 8. Cut the muslin along one of the dart Center Folds to within one inch of the point of the dart (Figure 139).

Take a four foot length of bias tape and pin the middle of it to the Waist at the Center Back. Continue to pin the bias tape to the Waist line out to the cut Dart Center Fold.

Take another four foot length of bias tape and pin it to the Waist line from the cut Dart Center Fold to the Side Seam.

These two lengths of bias tape will be used to adjust the back dart to the correct width.

Step 9. Put the muslin back on. Tie the first bias tape around the Waist and adjust it so that the Center Back of the muslin follows the Center Back of the body.

Step 10. Adjust the other bias tape by holding one end of the tape in the left hand and the other end in the right hand. Keep the upper arms close to the body. The muslin should be adjusted so that the fabric fits smoothly down the side of the back (Figure 140). Tie the bias tape around the Waist when the correct location is established. Be careful that your body is not twisted.

Step 11. Place a tape measure around your Waist and, by looking in the mirrors, determine the back Dart Width.

Step 12. Take the muslin off and remove the bias tapes. Mark half of the Dart Width on either side of the Dart Center Fold. Connect these marks to the top of the dart with straight lines.

Step 13. Baste the dart together and recheck the fit. Be careful that the Dart Width is not too large, creating excess fullness at the top of the dart. The Dart Width will normally be between one and two inches.

If no further adjustments are required, transfer the dart markings from the fitted side to the unfitted side and baste that dart. Check this dart for fit.

NECK CURVE

Figure 141

ARMHOLE CURVE

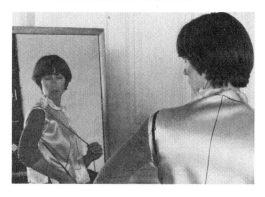

Figure 142

Step 14. Establish the Side Seam location on a fitted undergarment. Place a pin at the top of the desired Side Seam, another pin near the Waist, and one pin at right angles to the Side Seam line.

Step 15. Put the muslin on and adjust the back so that the Center Back is located correctly. Smooth the fabric of the back on the left side using the right hand. Keep the upper arms close to the sides of your body. With a felt tip marker, indicate the location of the three pins from the fitted undergarment.

Step 16. Repeat this same procedure for the front pattern. Take the muslin off and draw in the Side Seams. The pin that was at right angles to the Side Seam will be used to line up the front and back patterns at the correct height.
Baste the Side Seams together and check the fit.

Step 17. After the fit is established, check the length of the front Armhole Curve against the length of the back Armhole Curve. Adjust the Side Seams forwards or backwards until they are exactly the same length (see Step 14, page 61).

Step 18. Add the ease back in at the top of the Side Seam. The distance from the Center Front to the Side Seam to the Center Back should be two inches plus one-half the Chest measurement for men and two inches plus one-half the Full Bust measurement for women. Add the ease in equal amounts to the front and the back pattern.

Step 19. To mark the Neck Curve, put the muslin on and place the typewriter ribbon around the neck (Figure 141). Pull it back and forth slightly to leave a line of ink on the back pattern. The front Neck Curve may be drawn in with a felt tip pen.

Step 20. The Armhole Curve may be marked by placing the typewriter ribbon around the arm (Figure 142). Make sure that the ribbon is positioned correctly on the Shoulder Point and pull it back and forth slightly to leave a line of ink. The front Armhole Curve may be marked with a felt tip pen.

Step 21. Place a string around the Waist at the correct height. Use the typewriter ribbon to mark the back Waist line. Use a felt tip pen to mark the front Waist line.

Fitting the Skirt on Yourself

The procedure used to fit the skirt may also be used to fit the pants.

Step 1. Put the muslin skirt on and pin the Hip line securely to hold it in place.

Step 2. Shape in the front darts for women as described on page 31. Remove the muslin and transfer the marks from the fitted side to the unfitted side. Baste the front darts and check the fit.

Step 3. The point of the buttock dart will be determined next. Stand with your back lightly against the wall. You will be able to feel where your body bends away from the wall in both a horizontal and a vertical direction. The point where these two curves meet will be the point of the dart. Mark it with a felt tip pen.

Step 4. Take the muslin off and draw a line parallel to the Center Back line from the point of the dart to the Waist. This will be the Center Fold of the dart. Cut along this line to within one inch of the point of the dart.

Step 5. Pin a four foot length of bias tape to the Waist of the skirt. Pin the middle of the tape at the Center Back and continue pinning to the Dart Center Fold. Pin another length of bias tape from the Dart Center Fold to the Side Seam.

Step 6. Put the muslin skirt on and adjust the Center Back to the correct location. Tie the Center Back in place with the bias tape.

Step 7. Adjust the other bias tape so that the fabric fits smoothly on the side of the hip. Tie it in place. Place a tape measure around the Waist and measure the Dart Width.

Step 8. Remove the muslin and take off the bias tapes. Mark off half of the Dart Width on either side of the Dart Center Fold. Draw in the shape of the dart. Transfer the markings from the fitted side to the unfitted side. Baste the darts and check the fit.

Step 9. Shape in the Side Seams from the Hips to the Waist. This will be fairly easy to do because the upper torso may be twisted somewhat without shifting the lower torso. Make sure the the Center Front and Center Back are in place.

Step 10. Take off the muslin and draw in the Side Seams. Add the ease back in at the Hip line. Transfer the marks from the fitted side to the unfitted side. Baste the Side Seams and check the fit.

Step 11. The Hip line must be kept parallel to the floor while the Waist is drawn in. Tie a string around the Waist to hold the skirt in place. With a yardstick, measure from the floor to the Hip line. Adjust the skirt up or down so that this measurement is the same around the entire body.

Use the typewriter ribbon to mark the back of the Waist. Use a felt tip pen to mark the front of the Waist.

THE BASIC SLEEVE

THE ARM

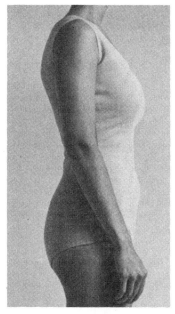

Figure 143

SHAPE OF ELBOW

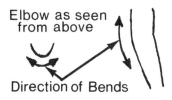

Elbow as seen from above

Direction of Bends

Figure 144

THE PATTERN AND THE BODY

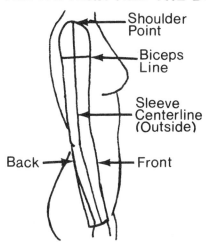

Shoulder Point

Biceps Line

Sleeve Centerline (Outside)

Back — Front

Figure 145

The sleeve presented here is a fairly simple pattern that will require little if any fitting. There are two versions of the basic sleeve. First the fundamental shape of the sleeve will be drafted. The second version will include a dart at the elbow for closely fitted sleeves. Deciding which of these two patterns to use will depend on the desired design.

The Body and the Sleeve

The arm may be divided into three parts for pattern drafting purposes. The upper part is where the arm joins into the body. The portion of the pattern which covers this part of the arm is called the Sleeve Cap. The second part of the arm is the upper arm. This is basically cylindrical in shape. And the last part is the lower arm, from the elbow to the wrist, which is also cylindrical in shape.

The upper arm and the lower arm are joined together by the elbow. Notice that the lower arm bends forward slightly at the elbow as the arm hangs naturally down at the side.

This bend at the elbow has two important effects on sleeve patterns. First, the back of the arm will be longer than the front of the arm. Secondly, a tightly fitted sleeve must have a dart at the elbow to compensate for the bend. The fabric must bend horizontally around the arm and vertically the fabric must bend from the upper arm to the lower arm (Figure 144). Loose fitting sleeves will not require this dart. The arm, in this case, may be treated as one continuous cylinder.

The arm and the resulting sleeve pattern may also be divided vertically into a front, outside, back, and inside. These vertical divisions will be important later when various sleeve designs are created.

The Sleeve Pattern

There will be two basic reference lines for the sleeve. The first will be a straight line down the outside of the arm. This line will start at the Shoulder Point and will be called the Sleeve Centerline. The second basic reference line will divide the pattern into a Sleeve Cap portion and an Arm portion. This line will be at right angles to the Sleeve Centerline and will be called the Biceps line.

Measurements:

#32) Arm Length _____

#34) Sleeve Cap _____

#12) Biceps _____

#14) Palm _____

#33) Shoulder to Elbow _____

BASIC REFERENCE LINES

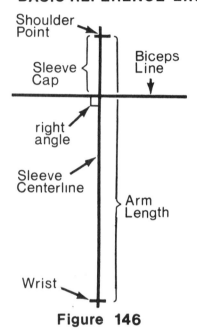

Figure 146

THE ARM

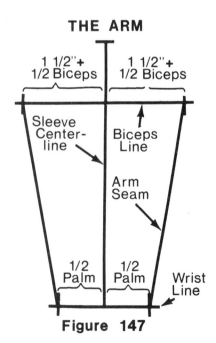

Figure 147

THE BASIC REFERENCE LINES

Step 1. In the middle of a sheet of paper, draw a vertical line and mark off the Arm Length measurement (#32). This is the Sleeve Centerline (Figure 146). The top of this length is the Shoulder Point. The bottom will be the Wrist.

Step 2. On the Sleeve Centerline measure down the Sleeve Cap length (#34). From this point draw a line at right angles to the Sleeve Centerline. This is the Biceps line.

Note - The Sleeve Cap length should normally be between five and six inches. If your measurement differs from this, recheck it carefully.

THE ARM PORTION

Step 3. On the Biceps line mark off one and one-half inch plus one-half the Biceps measurement (#12) to either side of the Sleeve Centerline (Figure 147).

The Sleeve Centerline will divide the pattern in half. The one and one-half inches on either side of the Sleeve Centerline is the basic fitting ease.

Step 4. At the bottom of the Arm Length measurement draw a line at right angles to the Sleeve Centerline. This is the Wrist line. On the Wrist line mark off half of the Palm measurement (#14) to either side of the Sleeve Centerline.

The Palm measurement is used at the Wrist line to indicate how big the pattern must be for the hand to get through the sleeve.

Step 5. Connect the marks on the Biceps line to the marks on the Wrist line to establish the Arm Seam of the sleeve.

THE SLEEVE CAP

The line of the Sleeve Cap seam may be drafted by using the following technique. It is a standard geometric shape that works very well for most people without any fitting.

Step 6. Divide the Biceps line into six equal parts. Draw lines at right angles to the Biceps line from each of these points (Figure 148).

Step 7. Draw two diagonal lines from the Shoulder Point to the ends of each side of the Biceps line.

SLEEVE CAP

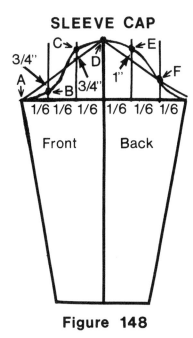

Figure 148

SLEEVE CAP ADJUSTING

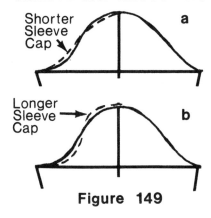

Figure 149

SEAM LINE ADJUSTING

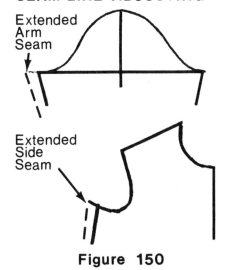

Figure 150

Step 8. Mark points A, B, C, D, E, F, and G as indicated in Figure 148. Point A is at the end of the Biceps line. Point B is three-quarters of an inch below the diagonal line. Point C is three-quarters of an inch above the diagonal line. Point D is at the Shoulder Point. Point E is one inch above the diagonal line. Point F is on the diagonal line. And point G is at the end of the Biceps line.

Step 9. Draw in the Sleeve Cap line by connecting these points. Notice that the Sleeve Cap has a front side and a back side. Mark your pattern accordingly.

The front curve of the Sleeve Cap is more pronounced from point C to point A than the back curve between point E and point G. This is because the curve of the body is more pronounced in the front than it is in the back.

THE SLEEVE CAP LENGTH

The length of the Sleeve Cap curve must be compared to the length of the Armhole Curve because these two lines will be sewn together.

Step 10. On the front bodice pattern measure the length of the Armhole Curve and note this length.

Step 11. On the Sleeve Pattern measure the length of the front Sleeve Cap Curve from the Shoulder Point to the Biceps line. This curve should be one-half an inch longer than the front Armhole Curve.

For Minor Adjustments - The length of the Sleeve Cap may be adjusted by changing its shape. A shallower curve will make the length shorter (Figure 149a). A more pronounced curve will make the length longer (Figure 149b).

For Major Adjustments - If the Sleeve Cap is shorter than it should be, extend out the Arm seam (Figure 150a). If the Sleeve Cap is longer than it should be, extend out the Side Seam of the Bodice (Figure 150b).

The bodice is expanded rather than making the sleeve smaller because the basic fitting ease must be maintained around the arm.

Step 12. Repeat these same procedures for the back Bodice pattern and the back of the Sleeve Cap using the same measurements.

SLEEVE CAP EASE

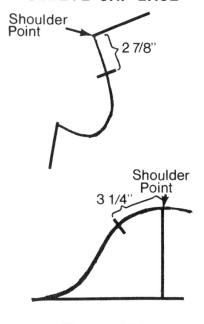

Figure 151

ELBOW DART

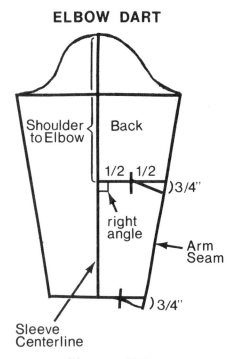

Figure 152

SLEEVE CAP EASE

The Sleeve Cap line is made larger than the Armhole Curve so that the sleeve may be eased into the body of the garment. This allows the fabric of the sleeve at the top of the arm to shape over the curve of the shoulder. The following procedure will place the ease in the proper part of the sleeve.

Step 13. On the front Armhole Curve of the bodice measure two and seven-eighths inches from the Shoulder Point and make a mark (Figure 151).

Step 14. On the front portion of the Sleeve Cap curve measure three and one-quarter inches from the Shoulder Point and make a mark.

These two points will be lined up during the sewing procedure as will the Shoulder Points to create three-eighths of an inch in the front Sleeve Seam.

Step 15. Repeat the procedure for the back using the same measurements. The back of the sleeve and the bodice are commonly marked with two notches to indicate the back. The front commonly has one notch. This keeps the left sleeve from being put into the right armhole.

THE ELBOW DART

Step 16. On the Sleeve Centerline measure down the Shoulder to Elbow length (#33) and make a mark (Figure 152). From this point draw a line at right angles to the Sleeve Centerline towards the back side of the sleeve. This is the Elbow line.

Step 17. On the Elbow line divide the sleeve in half between the Sleeve Centerline and the Arm Seam and make a mark. This establishes the point of the elbow dart.

Step 18. On the Arm Seam measure down three-quarters of an inch from the Elbow line. Connect this mark to the point of the dart.

The dart, as it is now drawn, removes fabric from the Arm Seam. Fabric must be added back to the length of the seam below the Wrist line to keep the two Arm Seams the same length.

Step 19. Extend the Arm Seam down three-quarters of an inch and mark the new length.

Step 20. Divide the Wrist measurement in half between the Sleeve Centerline and the Arm Seam to find the back of the arm on the Wrist line. Curve the Wrist line from this point to the new extended Arm Seam length.

WRIST LINE

Sleeve Without Dart

1/2"

Sleeve With Dart

1/2"

Figure 153

CURVING THE WRIST LINE

Put a rubber band around the biceps so that it is parallel to the floor. Now measure down the front of the arm and down the back of the arm (see Figure 145). You will notice that the front is one inch shorter than the back.

The Wrist line may be shaped to correspond to this difference. This curved shape may be added to either the sleeve pattern that has an elbow dart or to the sleeve pattern that does not have an elbow dart.

Step 21. Divide the Wrist line into four equal parts and mark the front and the back. Make the front wrist half an inch shorter than the existing Wrist line and the back wrist half an inch longer. Curve the Wrist line to blend these points together (Figure 153).

Fitting the Sleeve

The best way to fit this sleeve is to baste it into the armhole. Put the muslin on and check the fit. If the sleeve does not hang smoothly down the arm, pull the Sleeve Cap up at the seam line until it does. Pin the excess fabric out.

Take the muslin off. Take the basting out. Correct the Sleeve Cap line. Rebaste and check the fit once again.

There should be little adjustment required to this Sleeve Cap.

PATTERN ALTERATION TECHNIQUES

The basic patterns, after they have been fitted, show the shape of the body. These patterns may be changed to create an infinite number of designs.

To demonstrate some of these designs, this section shows how to make the patterns for standard contemporary garments. The principles used to achieve these patterns may be modified and applied to create original designs.

One of two things happens to patterns when they are altered. First, the position of the seam lines or the dart lines may be changed. Second, the patterns may be expanded to add more fullness to certain areas of the body. Most designs will use both of these changes.

PATTERN REDUCTION

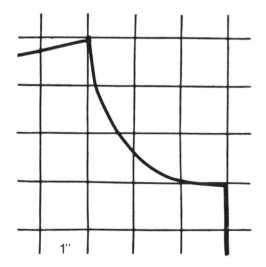

1"

1/4"

Figure 154

USING THIS SECTION

It will be best to practice the pattern alteration techniques as you read this section. If you use quarter scale patterns, many different designs may be created on a tablet of $8\frac{1}{2}$" x 11" tracing paper. These scaled down patterns may then be used as a reference to alter full sized patterns.

You may use the quarter scale patterns illustrated here, or you may reduce your own fitted patterns to quarter scale.

To reduce your fitted patterns to quarter scale, line off the full sized patterns with parallel lines spaced exactly one inch apart. Draw these lines in both horizontal and vertical directions. Next, take a piece of paper ruled off in quarter inch squares. Redraw the full sized pattern square by square onto the quarter ruled paper (Figure 154).

SETTING UP THE BASIC PATTERNS

During the alteration techniques, lines will be drawn on the basic patterns to establish new dart and seam locations. The basic patterns will then be traced to create the new designs. To protect the original patterns for repeated use, mount them on artists' mat board or on thin sheets of plywood and cover them with clear contact paper. The lines for the particular design may be drawn on this clear contact paper with a felt tip pen. After the design has been completed, the markings may be cleaned off with rubbing alcohol or lighter fluid.

The felt tip pens may leave some residue on the contact paper after many uses. Therefore, it is a good idea to cover the patterns with two layers of the clear contact paper. When the top layer becomes clouded, it may be peeled off from the bottom layer. Replace it with a new sheet.

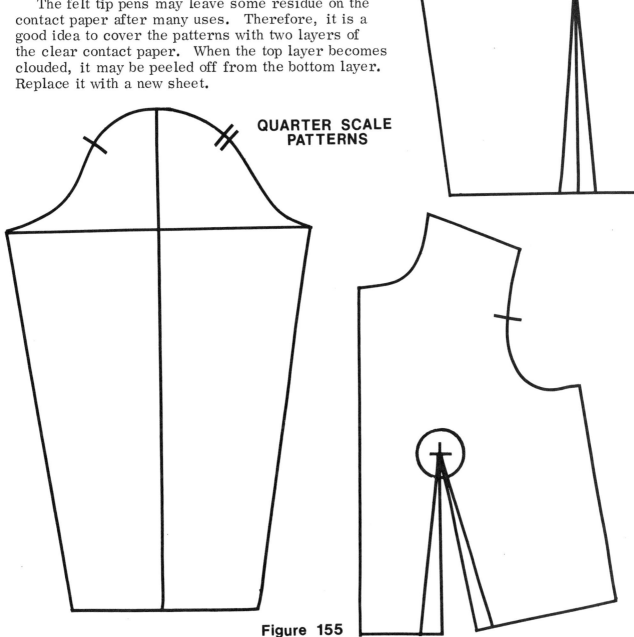

QUARTER SCALE PATTERNS

Figure 155

CHANGING SEAM LOCATIONS

Seam lines may be changed to different positions without affecting the fit of the basic patterns. There are two basic types of seam lines: external lines, and internal lines.

External lines define the edge of the garment. Raising or lowering a hem line on a dress or skirt changes the external line of the garment. Necklines are also external lines. Changing external lines does not affect the fit of the garment.

Internal lines are the seam lines seen on the body of the garment. These lines may or may not affect the fit. A yoke, for instance, on a man's shirt does not change the fit. It only changes the appearance of the garment by adding additional lines. The Princess Seam, on the other hand, usually adds not only new visual lines to the body, but it also may change how closely the garment follows the body.

Changing External Lines

CHANGING THE NECKLINE

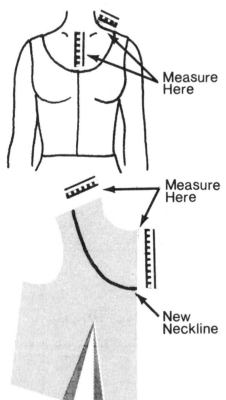

Measure Here

Measure Here

New Neckline

Figure 156

Variations of the neckline are shown on the opposite page. These variations may be achieved by simply drawing in the desired shape of the neckline on the pattern.

Figure 156 shows how the neckline may be changed on the basic pattern. The body is measured first and these measurements are placed on the pattern. Then the desired neckline may be drawn in.

THE PROCEDURE

Step 1. Measure down the body at Center Front to determine the desired depth of the neckline. Mark this length on the Center Front of the pattern.

Step 2. Measure on the shoulder how far out the neckline is to be. Mark this length on the Shoulder Seam on the basic pattern.

Step 3. Draw in the shape of the desired neckline.

Step 4. Place a piece of semi-transparent tracing paper over the basic pattern. Trace the basic pattern following the line of the new neckline.

NECKLINE VARIATIONS

These are variations of the neckline that may be created by following the same procedure. Simply measure the body to the location of the neckline. Mark the pattern accordingly and draw in the desired shape.

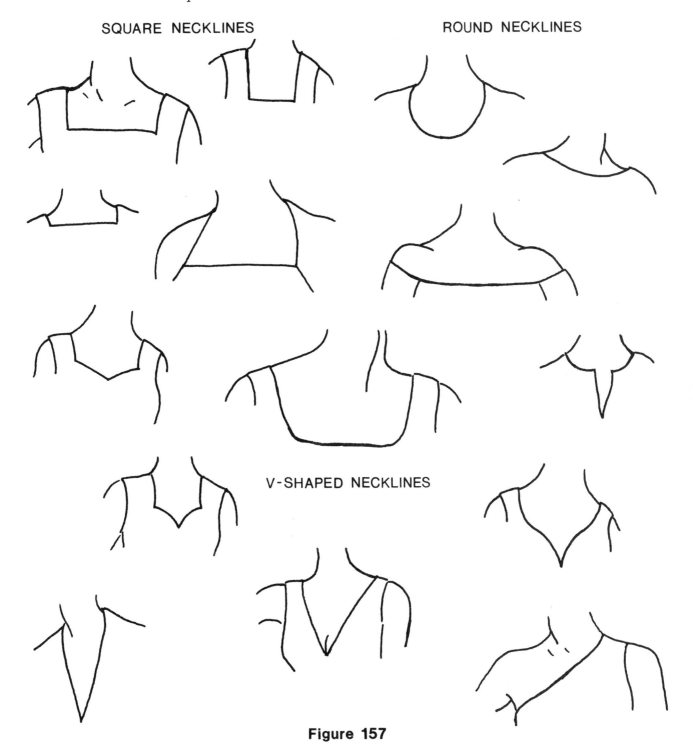

SQUARE NECKLINES

ROUND NECKLINES

V-SHAPED NECKLINES

Figure 157

Changing Internal Lines

THE CUTTING TECHNIQUE

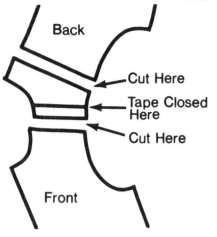

Figure 158

MEN'S YOKE PATTERN

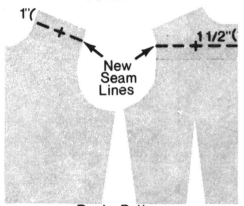

Basic Patterns

Traced Patterns

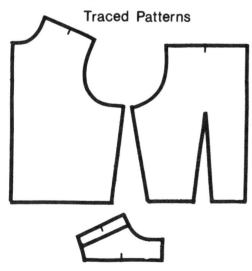

Figure 159

Altering internal seam lines which do not affect the fit of the body is primarily a process of cutting out the new seam lines and taping closed the seam lines that are to be removed. Figure 158 illustrates this principle for the yoke of a man's shirt.

Many variations in the appearance of garments are possible by adding this type of internal seam line to the design. The shirt illustrated in the lower right hand corner of Figure 160 has two vertical seams that have been added to the side front area.

These internal seam lines may be left as plain seams or their decorative value may be enhanced by making them flat-felled or corded seams. They may also be used to join contrasting fabric together.

The cutting principle illustrated in Figure 158 may be used to create the new patterns. However, because new seam allowances must be added to both sides of the cut seam the following procedure will save some time and trouble. This procedure describes specifically how to add a yoke to a man's shirt but the process may be adapted to add new seam lines or remove undesired seam lines on any garment.

THE PROCEDURE

Step 1. Determine the location of the new seam lines by measuring the body. The measurements given in Figure 159 are for a conventional man's yoke.

Step 2. Draw the new seam lines onto the basic patterns. Include seam alignment notches.

Step 3. Place a piece of semi-transparent tracing paper over the basic patterns.

Step 4. Trace around the front pattern starting at the new seam line. Do not trace the front yoke.

Step 5. Trace around the back pattern starting at the new seam line. Do not trace the back yoke.

Step 6. On a small piece of tracing paper, trace the back yoke indicated on the basic pattern.

Step 7. Line the traced back yoke up with the front yoke indicated on the basic pattern at the Shoulder Seam. Trace the front yoke.

Step 8. Add seam allowances around all of the patterns.

MEN'S SHIRT YOKES

These are variations of men's shirts that may all be created by following the procedure described on page 80. Always measure the body to determine the desired location of the seam locations and apply these measurements to the basic patterns.

Figure 160

CHANGING DART LOCATIONS

WOMAN'S FRONT PATTERN

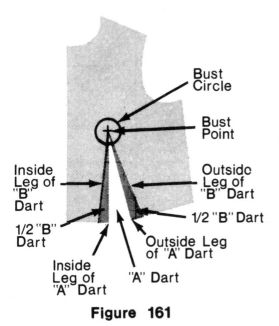

Figure 161

The dart is a wedge that is removed from the fabric to allow the fabric to bend smoothly in two directions at the same time. To illustrate how the dart may be changed, the woman's bust dart will be shifted to various locations.

To review briefly the function and the shape of the bust dart, look at Figure 161. The bust dart on the basic pattern is made up of two parts. The middle unshaded part of the dart is referred to as the "A" Dart. This dart shapes the fabric for the Above the Bust contour of the body. The darker shaded area on either side of the "A" Dart is the "B" Dart. This dart shapes the fabric for the Below the Bust contour.

The contours of the bust were discussed on page 58. The effect of these contours on fabric was discussed on page 62.

The edges of the dart will be referred to as the Dart Legs. The Dart Legs which are closest to the Center Front will be called the Inside Legs and the Dart Legs which are closest to the Side Seam will be called the Outside Legs.

The pattern also shows the Bust Point and a circle, around the Bust Point, the Bust Circle. This circle shows how far away the point of the dart must be from the Bust Point. The procedure for determining the size of the Bust Circle was described on page 58.

"A" DART AT SIDE

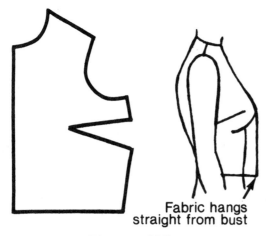

Fabric hangs straight from bust

Figure 162

"A" SIDE DART & "B" DART AT WAIST

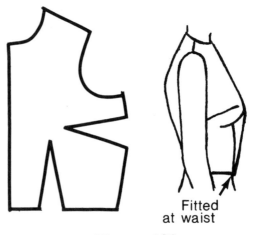

Fitted at waist

Figure 163

THE CUTTING TECHNIQUE

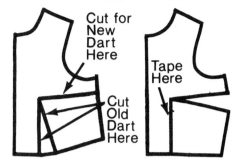

Figure 164

PREPARE THE BASIC

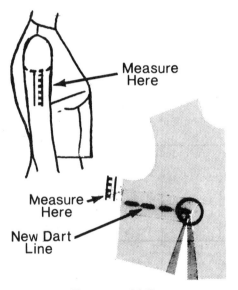

Figure 165

TRACE TO NEW DART

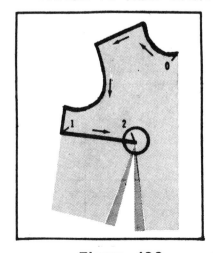

Figure 166

The "A" Dart shapes and the "B" Dart shapes may be combined into one bust dart, as was done for the basic pattern, or they may be divided into several darts.

Similarly the two dart shapes may be changed to any seam line on the front pattern. Page 51 illustrated how the line of the sewn dart may be changed to different directions without affecting the shape of the fabric.

The most common dart alteration is to change the shape of the "A" Dart to a seam other than the waist thus allowing the Waist line to coincide with the horizontal grain of the fabric. Figure 162 shows what happens when the "A" Dart is changed to the Side Seam. The "B" Dart shape may either be left as fullness in the garment, or it may be sewn out to shape the fabric in at the waist (Figure 163).

To understand how the dart shape may be changed, make a copy of the scaled down basic pattern and cut out the wedge of the "A" Dart (Figure 164). Cut a line for a new dart to the Bust Point. When the old dart is taped closed, this automatically shifts the dart wedge to the new location.

The cutting technique illustrates the principle involved in altering the dart location. However, once again, the tracing technique will be described because it is more economical of both time and material.

PREPARING THE BASIC PATTERN

Step 1. The first step in changing the location of the bust dart must be to determine the line of the new dart. To find the exact location of the side dart, measure down from the armpit to the desired height of the new dart. Mark this length on the Side Seam of the basic pattern (Figure 165). Draw a line from this mark to the Bust Point.

TRACE TO THE NEW DART

Step 2. Place a piece of tracing paper on top of the basic pattern.

Step 3. At the top of the Center Front line make a mark and label it "0" (Figure 166). Trace from this point around the pattern to the line of the new dart. Mark a "1" at this point.

Step 4. Trace the line of the new dart and mark a "2" at the end of this line.

TRACE TO OLD DART

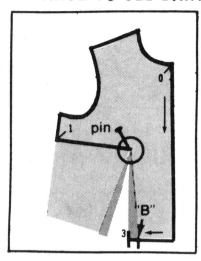

Figure 167

PIVOT AND COMPLETE

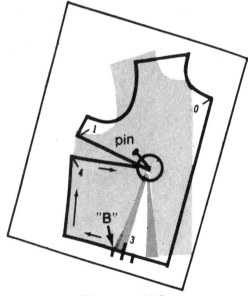

Figure 168

ADDING THE "B" DART

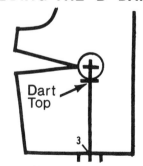

Figure 169

TRACE TO THE OLD DART

Step 5. Go back to the "0" and trace around the pattern to the Inside Leg of the "A" dart (the dart that is to be moved). Mark a "3" at this point. Also indicate the Inside Leg of the "B" dart on the Waist line (Figure 167).

PIVOT AND COMPLETE

Step 6. Mark the Bust Point on the tracing paper. This will be the pivot point. Put a pin through both the tracing paper and the basic pattern at this point.

Step 7. Pivot the tracing paper so that point "3" touches the Outside Leg of the "A" dart (Figure 168). This step removes the wedge of the dart from the Waist line.

Step 8. After the pivot, trace from point "3" to the line of the new dart on the basic pattern. Mark this point "4". Also make a mark indicating where the Outside Leg of the "B" dart is on the Waist line.

Step 9. Make a mark where the Bust Circle crosses the line drawn from point "1" to point "2". Connect this mark to point "4" to create the bottom leg of the new dart.

ADDING THE "B" DART

Not all designs will require the "B" dart. Those that do may use the following procedure to draw in the "B" dart to the Waist line.

Step 10. Draw a line straight down from the Bust Point to point "3" on the Waist line (Figure 169). This is the fold line of the dart.

Step 11. Find where the fold line crosses the Bust Circle and make a mark. This is the top of the dart.

Step 12. On the Waist line, find the marks that indicate the Inside Leg and the Outside Leg of the "B" dart. Connect these points to the top of the dart (Figure 170).

THE "B" DART

Figure 170

THE DART END

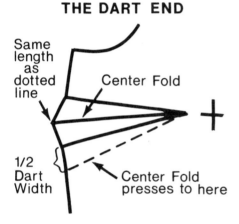

Same
length
as
dotted
line

Center Fold

1/2
Dart
Width

Center Fold
presses to here

Figure 171

SHAPING DARTS

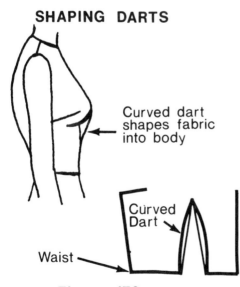

Curved dart
shapes fabric
into body

Curved
Dart

Waist

Figure 172

THE DART END

The end of the dart must be shaped so that the center fold of the dart will be long enough to be caught by the stitching at the Side Seam after the dart has been pressed in place.

Step 1. Draw in the center fold of the dart half way between the two dart legs (Figure 171).

Step 2. Draw a dotted line where the center fold of the dart will be pressed to. This will be half a Dart Width down the Side Seam.

Step 3. Measure the length of the dotted fold line from the point of the dart to the Side Seam. Mark this length on the center fold line that is between the dart legs. This establishes the correct length for the fold line.

Step 4. Connect the end of the fold line to the ends of the dart legs. This determines the shape of the end of the dart.

This same procedure may be used to draw in the end of any dart.

SHAPING DARTS

Each new dart location on the body provides the possiblity of adding subtle shaping details. The dart from the bust to the waist, for instance, may be curved as shown in Figure 172 so that the fabric will follow closer to the shape of the body. These variations should be determined during the final fitting of the garment.

CENTER FRONT DART

The dart to the Center Front seam is rarely if ever used as illustrated below. However, this pattern will be the basis for the cowl neckline described in the section on collars and necklines.

Notice that the basic pattern is traced to the Outside Leg of the dart first instead of to the Inside Leg as before.

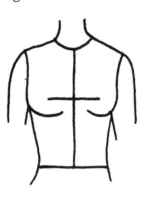
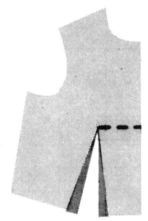

Prepare the
Basic Pattern

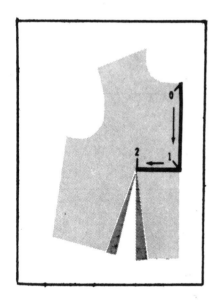

Trace to
New Dart

Trace to
Old Dart

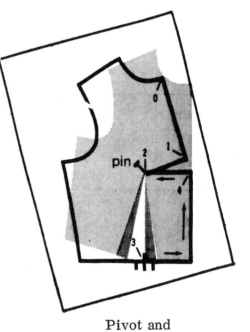

Pivot and
Complete

Figure 173

FRENCH DART

The French Dart may be drafted to either the intersection of the Waist line and the Side Seam or to just below this intersection.

To determine the exact location of the dart, the Side Seam for the particular garment being created must be drawn in first with the desired design ease.

This example shows one inch of design ease added to the Bust measurement and two inches added to the Waist. The procedure for establishing design ease for different types of garments is described in the section on designing garments.

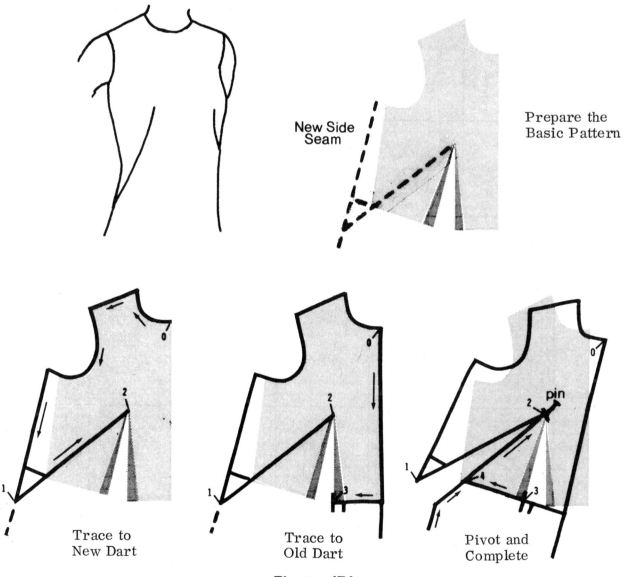

New Side Seam

Prepare the Basic Pattern

Trace to New Dart

Trace to Old Dart

Pivot and Complete

Figure 174

CURVED DART

The pattern described below illustrates two principles. First, it shows how to create a curved dart. Second, it shows what happens to the patterns when the entire dart is removed from the Waist line.

Notice in the final pattern how the Waist line curves down on the side. The Waist line on this design will not line up with the grain of the fabric. Therefore, there must be a seam at the waist. The waist seam will appear straight on the body because the dart will pull the fabric up under the bust. The effect of this is to create a fitted bust to waist area.

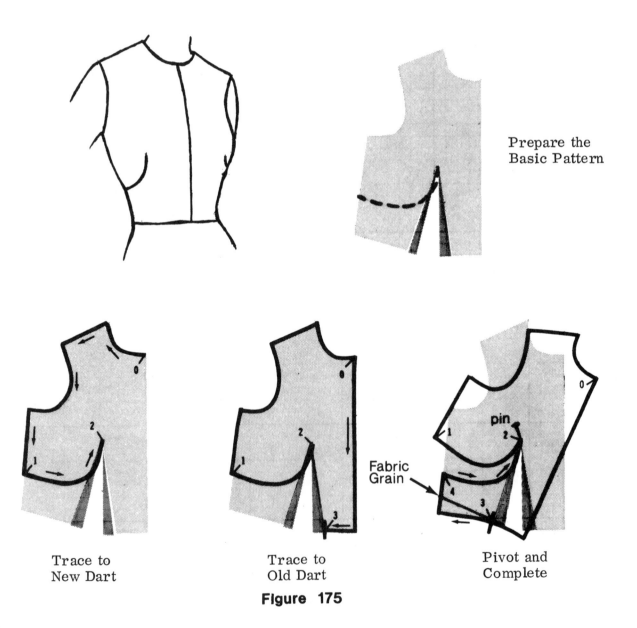

Prepare the
Basic Pattern

Trace to
New Dart

Trace to
Old Dart

Fabric
Grain

pin

Pivot and
Complete

Figure 175

SHOULDER DARTS

The single dart of the basic pattern may also be changed to multiple darts as illustrated below. To prepare the basic pattern for this change, draw in the desired new dart lines. Divide the "A" Dart Width into as many dart widths as there are new darts. The pattern will be pivoted so that an equal portion of the basic dart width will be distributed to each of the new darts.

In addition to adding multiple darts, the pattern shown here also has the Shoulder Seam lowered in front. The portion of the pattern taken off the front will be added to the back pattern.

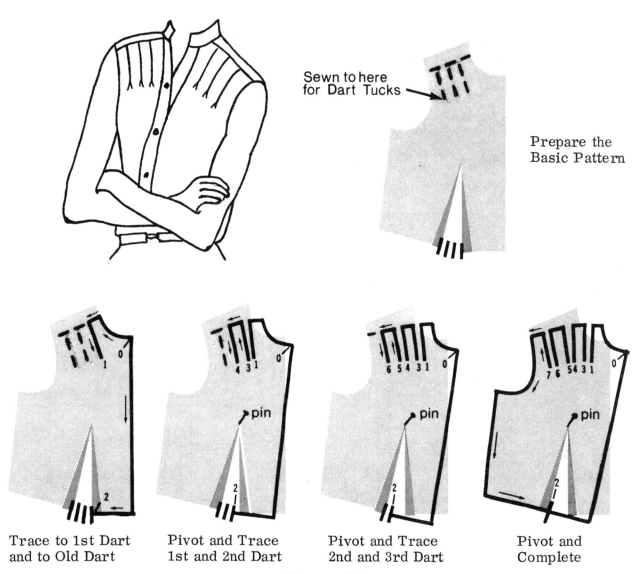

Sewn to here for Dart Tucks

Prepare the Basic Pattern

Trace to 1st Dart and to Old Dart

Pivot and Trace 1st and 2nd Dart

Pivot and Trace 2nd and 3rd Dart

Pivot and Complete

Figure 176

SHOULDER GATHERS

The Dart Width determines the shape of the garment. However, it does not always have to be sewn into a dart. The Dart Width may be held in the correct location by gathers, smocking or shirring.

The following illustration shows the basic pattern being changed to a design using gathers. First, the Shoulder Seam is dropped on the front pattern. Then the "A" dart is changed to the new Shoulder Seam. The top of the dart is closed by drawing an arc across it. The radius of the arc is the distance from the Bust Point to the Shoulder Seam. The front Shoulder Seam will be evenly gathered into the back Shoulder Seam.

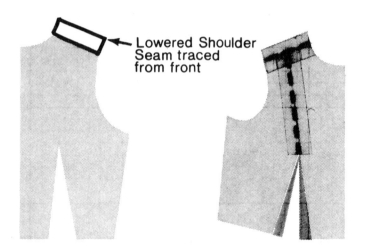

Lowered Shoulder Seam traced from front

Prepare the Basic Pattern

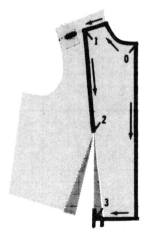

Trace to New Dart and to Old Dart

Pivot and Complete

Blend the Dart Width

Figure 177

90

VARIATIONS FOR SHOULDER GATHERS

The designs shown here may all be made using the pattern alteration procedure described on the preceding page.

The variations are achieved by changing the height of the Shoulder Seam, using different openings for the garments, and adding different sleeve and collar styles.

Figure 178

CHANGING DARTS TO SEAMS

PREPARE THE BASIC

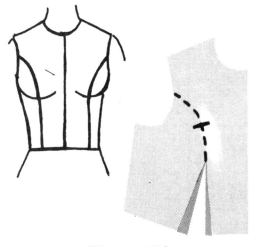

Figure 179

TRACE THE FRONT

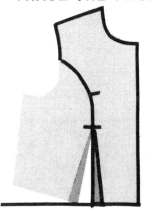

Figure 180

TRACE THE SIDE

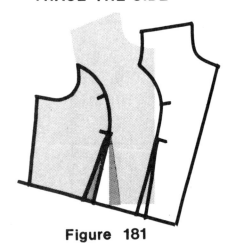

Figure 181

Darts may be changed to seams as long as the seam passes through or very close to the Bust Point. The classic seam line that illustrates this procedure is the Princess Seam.

PREPARE THE BASIC PATTERN

Step 1. Draw in the desired seam line on the basic pattern (Figure 179). Include seam alignment marks.

TRACE THE FRONT SECTION

Step 2. Place a piece of tracing paper over the basic pattern and trace the front section (Figure 180). Trace the inside leg of the "B" dart.

Step 3. Extend the Waist line out at right angles to the Center Front line.

TRACE THE SIDE SECTION

Step 4. Shift the tracing paper so that the extended Waist line of the traced front section lines up with the Waist line of the side section (Figure 181). Allow enough room between the patterns for seam allowances.

Step 5. Trace the side section including the outside leg of the "B" dart.

The basic pattern is traced in this manner so that the Waist line of the design will line up with the grain line of the fabric. When the tracing paper is shifted, this automatically places the "A" dart shape above the bust. Figure 182 shows what would happen if the two sections were traced close together.

THE DART SHAPES

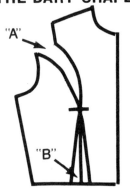

Figure 182

THE STRAIGHT PRINCESS SEAM

Another variation of the Princess Seam carries
the seam lines up to the shoulders instead of curving
them out to the armhole.

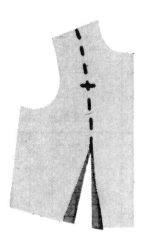

Prepare the
Basic Pattern

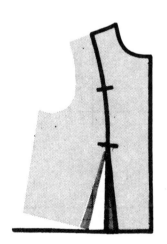

Trace the
Front Section

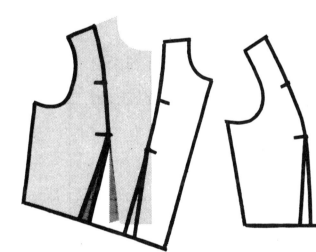

Trace the
Side Section

The Completed
Pattern

Figure   183

THE PRINCESS SEAM WITH A DART

This variation of the Princess Seam shows what happens when the seam lines do not go over the Bust Point. Additional shaping must be achieved by a small side dart.

To create this style, first shift the "A" dart to the Side Seam then use this new pattern as the basic pattern. Trace the front section and extend the Waist line. Trace the bottom part of the side section up to the dart and draw in the bottom leg of the dart. Remove the dart by shifting the tracing paper up so that the traced bottom leg of the dart coincides with the top leg of the dart on the basic pattern. Complete the tracing.

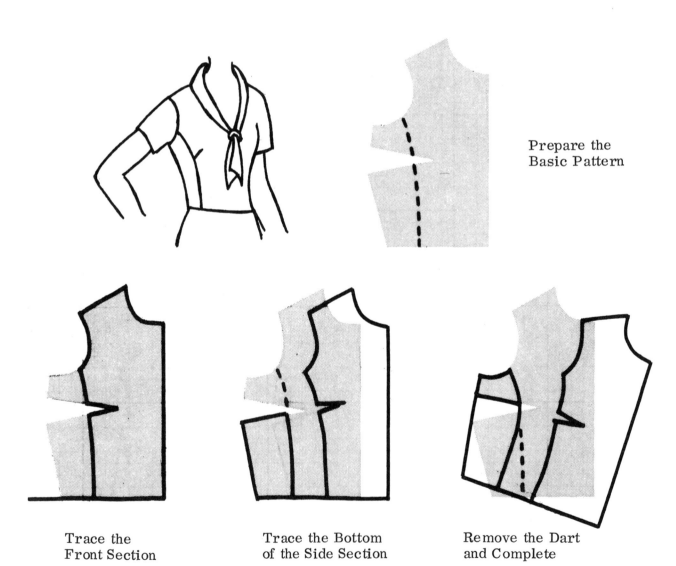

Prepare the
Basic Pattern

Trace the
Front Section

Trace the Bottom
of the Side Section

Remove the Dart
and Complete

Figure 184

PRINCESS SEAM VARIATIONS

The illustrations below show some of the different designs that may be created using the Princess Seam line.

Figure 185

FRONT YOKE

The darts may be changed to a variety of different seam lines as long as these lines cross over the Bust Point.

For the pattern shown below trace the yoke first. Shift the tracing paper up to allow room for seam allowances and trace the front section to the inside leg of the "A" dart. Extend the Waist line. Shift the tracing paper to remove the dart. The extended Waist line should be matched to the Waist line on the side of the basic pattern. The traced leg of the dart should coincide with the outside leg of the "A" dart on the basic pattern. Complete the pattern.

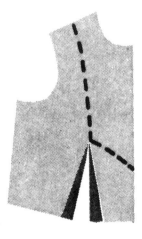

Prepare the
Basic Pattern

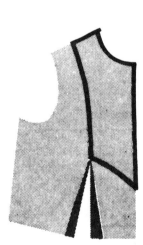

Trace the
Yoke

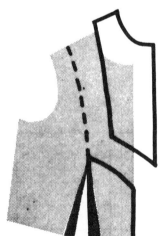

Trace the
Front Section

Remove the Dart
and Complete

Figure 186

FRONT SEAM VARIATIONS

To create original designs, relate the lines of the design to the body. Measure as necessary and draw the lines on the basic fitted patterns.

Use the "A" Dart Width for garments that are to hang freely from the bust, page 96. Use both the "A" and the "B" Dart Widths for garments that are to fit the waist as seen below.

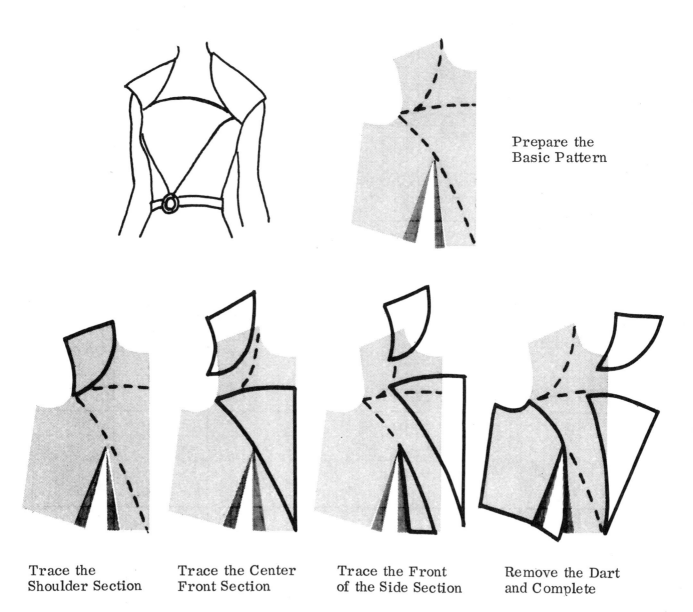

Prepare the Basic Pattern

Trace the Shoulder Section

Trace the Center Front Section

Trace the Front of the Side Section

Remove the Dart and Complete

Figure 187

THE BUST SEAM LINE

Some designs require a seam line to go straight around the bust, remaining parallel to the floor. To achieve this design, measure the distance from the Bust Point to the Waist line. Mark this length on the Side Seam and connect this mark to the Bust Point.

The seam line on the pattern must raise up like this because the fabric grain will drop down as it passes over the side of the bust (see page 62, Figure 125).

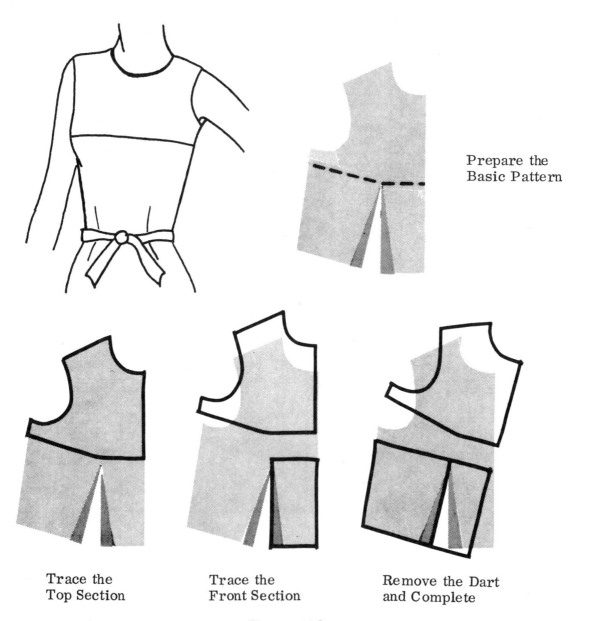

Prepare the
Basic Pattern

Trace the
Top Section

Trace the
Front Section

Remove the Dart
and Complete

Figure 188

THE YOKE FOR ROUNDED BACKS

The same principle seen on the previous page may be applied to the upper back dart for rounded backs. The shape of this dart may be changed to a yoke seam.

To achieve this design, draw a line parallel to the Waist line at the desired height of the yoke seam. Trace the bottom section of the pattern and shift the tracing paper down to allow room for seam allowances. Trace the Center Back section of the yoke to the inside leg of the upper dart and trace this leg. Shift the pattern so that the inside leg of the traced pattern coincides with the outside leg on the basic pattern. Complete the yoke pattern.

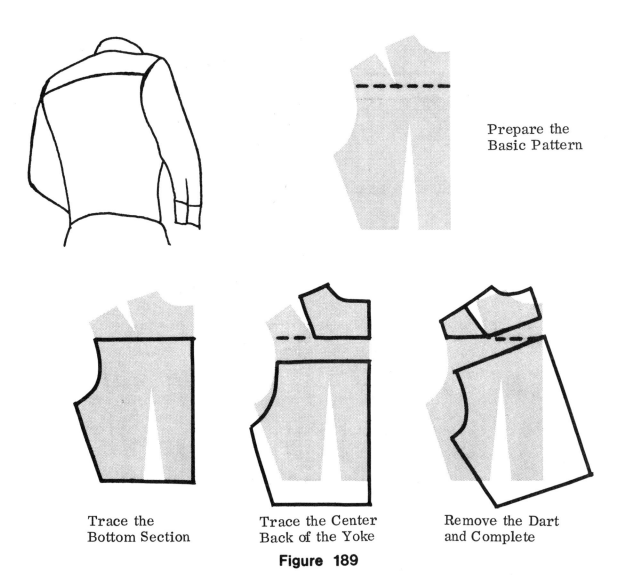

Prepare the
Basic Pattern

Trace the
Bottom Section

Trace the Center
Back of the Yoke

Remove the Dart
and Complete

Figure 189

ADDING FULLNESS

The fitted patterns follow the lines of the body. If a design requires that the garment not follow the body, the pattern must be expanded accordingly. Figure 190 shows the difference between the fitted skirt and a full skirt.

Further examples will be illustrated to show the principles of adding fullness to garments.

FITTED VERSUS FULL

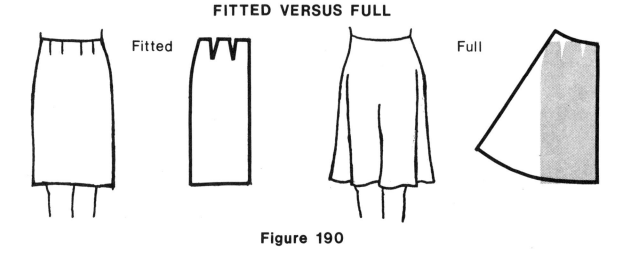

Figure 190

The Principles of Adding Fullness

LOCATION OF FULLNESS

Fullness will be located in a garment where the basic patterns are expanded. If the Side Seam is .expanded, then the fullness will appear on the side of the body. If the pattern is expanded in the middle, then there will be fullness in that portion of the body.

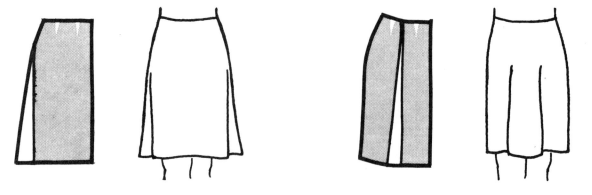

Figure 191

CHANGING DARTS TO FULLNESS

Darts may be changed to fullness by cutting through the center of the dart and down to the hem. The dart is then taped closed. The wedge of the dart now appears below the Hip line instead of above it.

If this new dart is sewn out, the skirt will be shaped exactly the same as the fitted skirt with the dart to the Waist line.

If this new dart is not sewn out, this wedge of extra fabric will appear as fullness in the skirt. The fullness will appear only in the skirt where it appears in the pattern, below the Hip line. The Waist to Hip area will still be fitted.

Another dart shaped wedge may be created by taping together the Side Seams of the front and the back pattern. This eliminates the Side Seam and creates fullness on the side of the body.

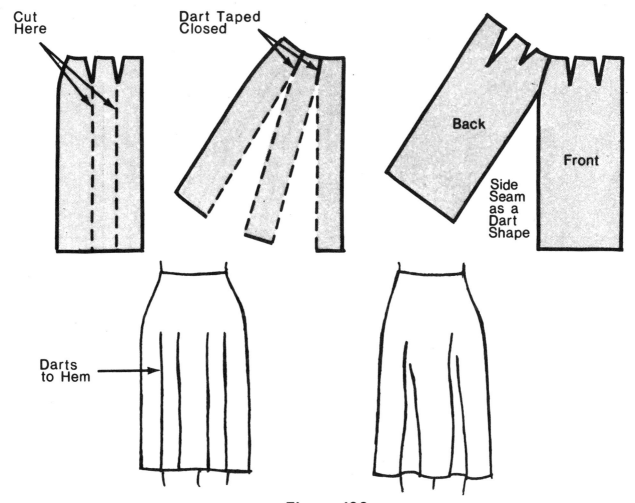

Figure 192

ADDING FULLNESS

To add fullness to the Waist to Hip area, the pattern must be cut in a number of sections and spread apart. Once again, the fullness will appear in the garment wherever the patterns are spread.

The pattern may be spread only at the hem with the waist remaining fitted, only at the waist with the hem remaining fitted, or the pattern may be expanded at both the waist and the hem.

Notice how the seam lines curve when fullness is added to one seam and not the other. If both seams are expanded then the seam lines will remain straight.

When the waist is expanded, the fabric will be gathered into a waistband.

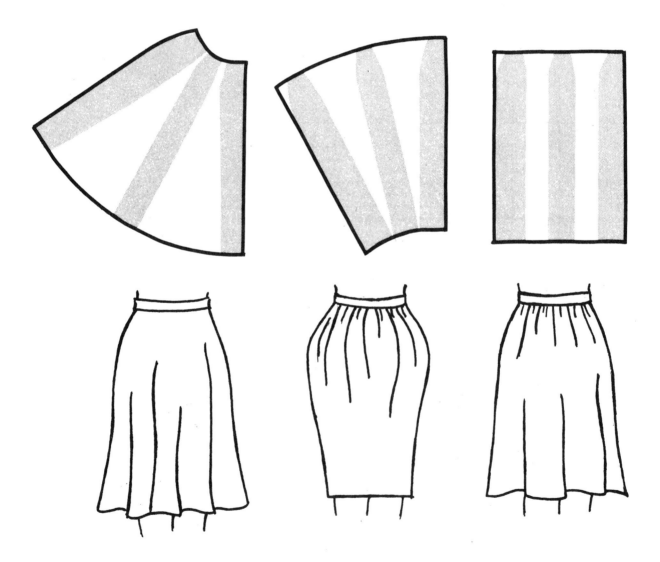

Figure 193

TRANSITIONS FROM FITTED TO FULL

If a single pattern piece is to go from fitted to full, the changes in the pattern piece cannot be too abrupt. To create a strong contrast from a fitted shape to a full shape one of two things may be done. Either the garment may be divided into several pattern pieces so that no one piece makes an extreme change. Or, a seam may be placed where the transition from fitted to full is to occur.

Notice that the curved seam fits smoothly into a straight seam of the same length to create fullness. A different kind of fullness is achieved by gathering a long straight seam into a shorter straight seam.

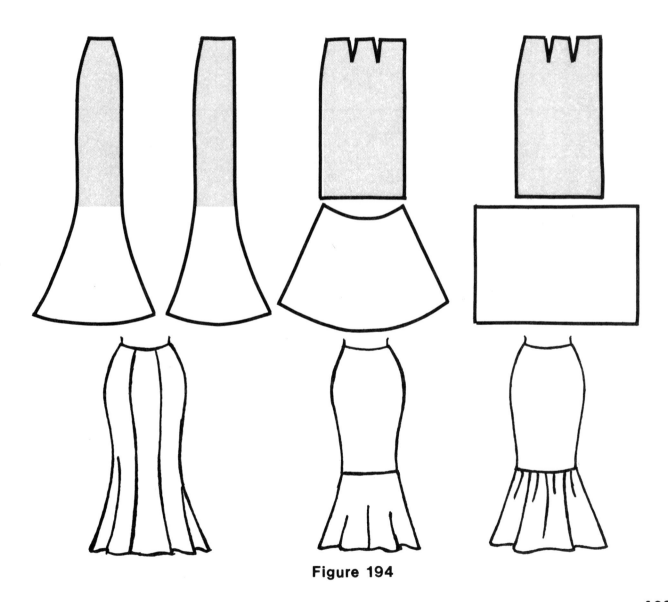

Figure 194

DETERMINING FULLNESS

The amount of fullness to use will depend on both the desired design and the nature of the fabric. Fullness added to stiff and/or heavy fabrics has a tendency to make the garment stand away from the body.

Light weight and/or supple fabric will drape into the body in graceful folds. More material will be required to obtain the same silhouette as the heavier fabric.

Taking the nature of the fabric into consideration, the following guidelines for fullness may be used.

Slight Fullness - Expand the fitted patterns so that they are half again larger than their fitted size. For example, a seam that is 12" long would be expanded to 18". This is usually the minimum amount of fullness that needs to be added to the patterns to be visually effective.

Medium Fullness - Expand the fitted patterns to twice their original size. For example, the 12" seam becomes 24".

Considerable Fullness - Expand the fitted patterns to three times their original size. The 12" seam would be 36". This is normally the maximum amount of fullness that can be added to the patterns without the garment becoming cumbersome.

Another way of approximating the desired amount of fullness is to lay out a tape measure to the desired size of the design. Shape the measure to include the fullness.

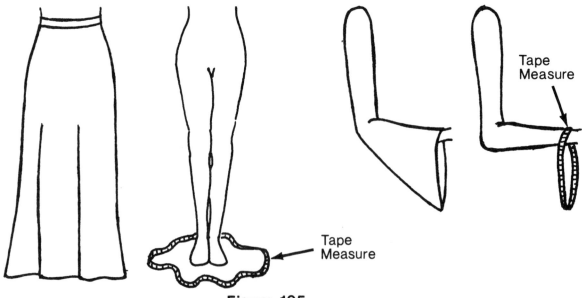

Tape Measure

Tape Measure

Figure 195

STRAIGHT SIDE FRONT

Three variations of the Princess Seam are shown here to illustrate subtle control of fullness.

The first Princess Seam line shows the Side Front seam being drawn straight down from the Bust Point. No fullness is added to the pattern at this point. Fullness is added to the Side Seam to allow for comfort of movement. This pattern would be appropriate for a coat.

Figure 196

FLARED SIDE FRONT

The second Princess Seam has fullness added to both sides of the Side Front line and to the Side Seam. This pattern would be appropriate for a dress that calls for fullness at the Side Front location of the body.

Notice that the Side Front line is shaped in to include part of the "B" dart. This will make the garment fit at the waist.

Figure 197

DECORATIVE SIDE FRONT

In the final variation of the Princess Seam the
Side Front line of the front pattern is shaped out to
the side. The Side Front line on the side pattern is
shaped in by the exact same amount. There has
been no fullness added to the Side Front. Instead
there will be a visual hourglass effect created. The
Side Front will shape into the waist and then back out
at the hem.

Figure 198

The Procedure for Adding Fullness

Adding Fullness to One Seam

PREPARE THE BASIC

Figure 199

TRACE THE FIRST SECTION

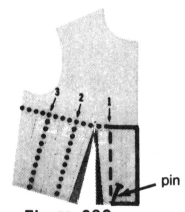

Figure 200

PIVOT AND TRACE

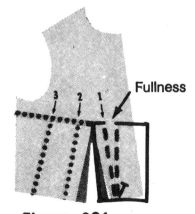

Figure 201

The procedure for adding fullness to garments will be described using the pattern for the woman's front bodice. The same technique may be used to add fullness to any of the basic patterns.

PREPARE THE BASIC PATTERN

Step 1. Indicate the location of the new seam lines on the basic pattern (Figure 199). In this case, the design that has the seam line going straight around the bust is going to be used (see page 98).

Step 2. Draw dotted lines on the basic pattern to indicate where the fullness is going to be added. These lines should be spaced frequently enough to ensure a smooth curve in the final pattern. Number these lines.

TRACE THE FIRST SECTION

Step 3. Place a sheet of tracing paper over the basic pattern. Trace the front section of the basic pattern to the first dotted line (Figure 200). Indicate the location of the dotted line with a series of dashes.

Step 4. Put a pin through both patterns on the seam that is not going to be expanded.

PIVOT AND TRACE

Step 5. Pivot the tracing paper to add the desired amount of fullness (Figure 201). In this case, the fullness will be half again as large as the basic pattern.
Measure the distance from the Center Front line to the first dotted line. Divide this measurement in half and pivot the pattern by this amount.

Step 6. Indicate the first dotted line of the basic pattern with dashes. Trace to the closest leg of the dart.

REMOVE THE DART

Step 7. Pivot out the "A" Dart shape (Figure 202). This step changes the dart shape to the new seam line (see page 98).

Step 8. Trace the basic pattern to the second dotted line and indicate this line with dashes.

Step 9. Put a pin through both patterns on the seam that is not going to be expanded.

REMOVE THE DART

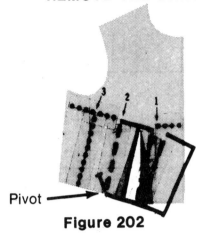

Pivot →

Figure 202

PIVOT AND TRACE

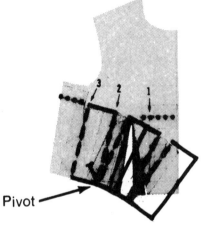

Pivot →

Figure 203

PIVOT AND TRACE

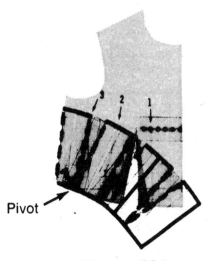

Pivot →

Figure 204

PIVOT AND TRACE

Step 10. Pivot the tracing paper to the desired amount of fullness (Figure 203).

Step 11. Indicate the second dotted line of the basic pattern with dashes and trace to the third dotted line. Indicate this line with dashes.

Step 12. Put a pin through both patterns at the seam that is not going to be expanded.

PIVOT AND TRACE

Step 13. Pivot the tracing paper to add the desired amount of fullness (Figure 204).

Step 14. Indicate the third dotted line with dashes and trace to the Side Seam.

Step 15. Indicate the Side Seam with dashes and put a pin through the seam line that is not going to be expanded.

PIVOT AND COMPLETE

Step 16. Pivot the tracing paper to add the desired amount of fullness and draw in the Side Seam (Figure 205).

Step 17. Shift the tracing paper down to allow room for seam allowances and trace the top portion of the pattern.

The fullness that has been added to the basic pattern is indicated by the diagonal lines in Figure 206. Notice that the top seam line is now one and a half times as long as its original dimension. This fullness will be gathered into the upper yoke. No fullness has been added to the bottom seam line.

When fullness is added to one seam and not the other seam line, the pattern must be curved in this manner.

PIVOT AND TRACE   THE PATTERN

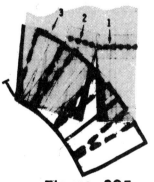

Figure 205   **Figure 206**

109

Adding Fullness to Two Seams

PREPARE THE BASIC

Figure 207

TRACE THE FIRST SECTION

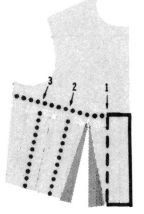

Figure 208

SHIFT AND TRACE

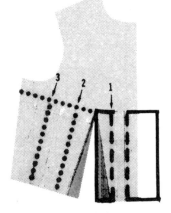

Figure 209

The procedure described here adds an equal amount of fullness to two seams. In this case the top and bottom seams of the previous design will be expanded to add half again as much fullness.

PREPARE THE BASIC PATTERN

Step 1. Indicate the location of any new seams on the basic pattern (Figure 207).

Step 2. Draw in dotted lines on the basic pattern to indicate where the fullness is going to be added.

TRACE THE FIRST SECTION

Step 3. Lay a sheet of tracing paper on the basic pattern. Trace the Center Front section to the first dotted line (Figure 208). Indicate the first dotted line with dashes.

SHIFT AND TRACE

Step 4. Shift the tracing paper to the side so that the desired fullness appears between the dashes on the tracing paper and the first dotted line on the basic pattern.

In this case, the pattern is shifted to add half again as much fullness to the basic pattern.

Step 5. Indicate the first dotted line with dashes and trace to the closest leg of the dart (Figure 209).

REMOVE THE DART

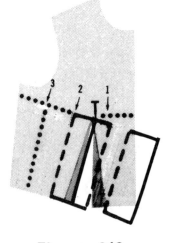

Figure 210

SHIFT AND TRACE

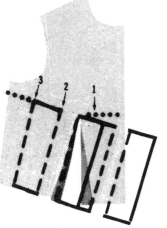

Figure 211

SHIFT AND TRACE

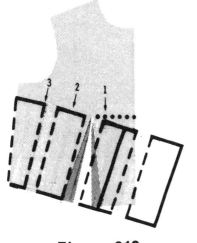

Figure 212

SHIFT AND COMPLETE

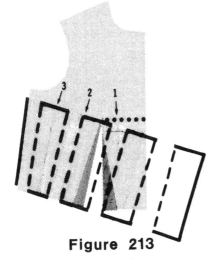

Figure 213

REMOVE THE DART

Step 6. Pivot out the "A" Dart shape (Figure 210). This step, once again, changes the dart shape to the new seam line.

Step 7. Trace to the second dotted line on the basic pattern and indicate this with dashes.

SHIFT AND TRACE

Step 8. Shift the tracing paper to the side to add the desired amount of fullness between the dashed line on the tracing paper and the dotted line on the basic pattern (Figure 211).

Step 9. Indicate the second dotted line with dashes and trace to the third dotted line of the basic pattern. Indicate the third dotted line with dashes.

SHIFT AND TRACE

Step 10. Shift the tracing paper to add the desired amount of fullness (Figure 212).

Step 11. Indicate the third dotted line with dashes and trace to the Side Seam. Indicate the Side Seam line with dashes.

SHIFT AND COMPLETE

Step 12. Shift the tracing paper to add the desired amount of fullness (Figure 213). Complete the pattern by tracing to the Side Seam on the basic pattern.

The fullness that has been added to the basic pattern is indicated by the diagonal lines in Figure 214.

When patterns are expanded to add the same amount of fullness to both seams, the pattern will be shifted in a straight manner as seen here.

THE PATTERN

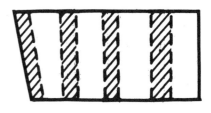

Figure 214

Adding Mixed Fullness

PREPARE THE BASIC

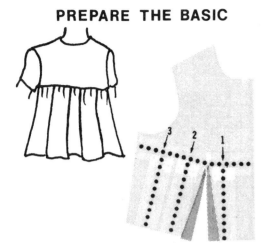

Figure 215

TRACE THE FIRST SECTION

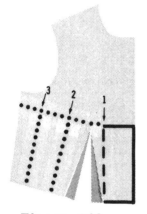

Figure 216

SHIFT THE PATTERN

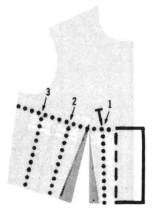

Figure 217

In some cases a design may require that some fullness be added to one seam and more fullness be added to the opposite seam. The following procedure may be used to achieve this effect.

PREPARE THE BASIC PATTERN

Step 1. Indicate the location of the new seam lines on the basic pattern (Figure 215).

Step 2. Draw in dotted lines to indicate where the fullness is to be added.

TRACE THE FIRST SECTION

Step 3. Place a piece of tracing paper over the basic pattern. Trace from the Center Front line to the first dotted line on the basic pattern (Figure 216). Indicate the location of this line with dashes.

SHIFT THE PATTERN

Step 4. Shift the tracing paper to the side to create the desired amount of fullness for the shorter seam (Figure 217).

In this case, the top seam will have half again as much fullness added.

Step 5. Put a pin through both patterns in this seam at the top of the first dotted line.

PIVOT AND TRACE

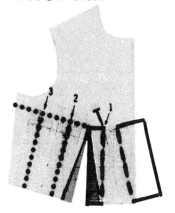

Figure 218

REMOVE THE DART

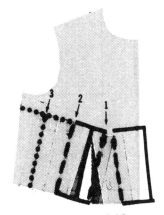

Figure 219

SHIFT THE PATTERN

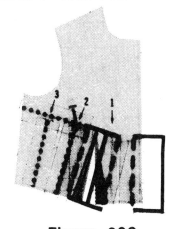

Figure 220

PIVOT AND TRACE

Step 6. Pivot the tracing paper to add the desired amount of fullness to the longer seam (Figure 218).

In this case, the length of the bottom seam line will be doubled.

Step 7. Indicate the location of the first dotted line of the basic pattern with dashes. Trace to the closest leg of the dart.

REMOVE THE DART

Step 8. Remove the dart and trace to the second dotted line on the basic pattern (Figure 219). Indicate this line with dashes.

SHIFT THE PATTERN

Step 9. Shift the tracing paper to the side to add the desired amount of fullness to the shorter seam line (Figure 220).

Step 10. Put a pin through both patterns in the shorter seam at the top of the second dotted line.

PIVOT AND TRACE

Step 11. Pivot the pattern to add the desired amount of fullness to the longer seam line (Figure 221).

Step 12. Indicate the second dotted line of the basic pattern with dashes and trace to the third dotted line. Indicate this line with dashes.

PIVOT AND TRACE

Figure 221

SHIFT THE PATTERN

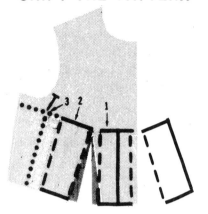

Figure 222

PIVOT AND TRACE

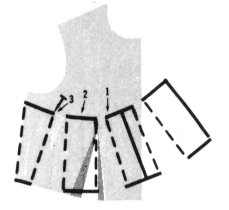

Figure 223

SHIFT THE PATTERN

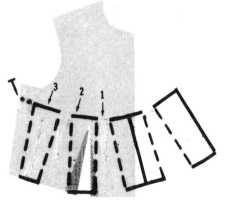

Figure 224

SHIFT THE PATTERN

Step 13. Shift the tracing paper to the side to add the desired amount of fullness to the shorter seam (Figure 222).

Step 14. Put a pin through both patterns on the shorter seam at the top of the third dotted line.

PIVOT AND TRACE

Step 15. Pivot the pattern to add the desired amount of fullness to the longer seam line (Figure 223).

Step 16. Indicate the third dotted line of the basic pattern with dashes and trace to the Side Seam. Indicate the Side Seam with dashes.

SHIFT THE PATTERN

Step 17. Shift the tracing paper to the side to add the desired amount of fullness to the shorter seam (Figure 224).

Step 18. Put a pin through the patterns at the top of the Side Seam.

PIVOT AND COMPLETE

Step 19. Pivot the pattern to add the desired amount of fullness to the longer seam line (Figure 225). Complete the tracing.

The diagonal lines in Figure 226 indicate where the fullness has been added to this pattern.

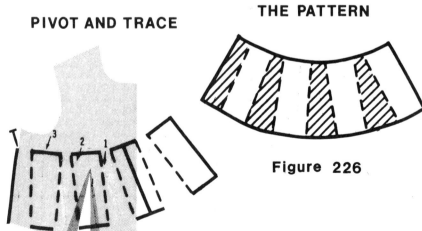

PIVOT AND TRACE

Figure 225

THE PATTERN

Figure 226

GATHERS FROM THE DART

The fullness for this design is created by shifting the shape of the dart to above the bust. The extra fabric from the shape of the dart will be gathered into the yoke. No additional fullness needs to be added to the basic patterns.

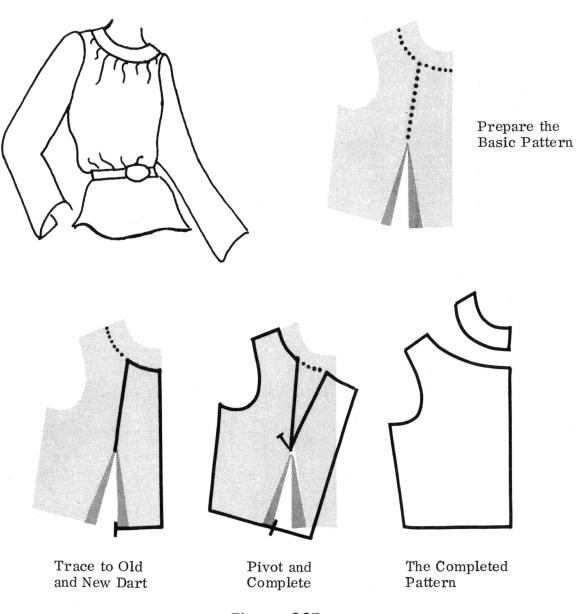

Prepare the
Basic Pattern

Trace to Old
and New Dart

Pivot and
Complete

The Completed
Pattern

Figure 227

115

GATHERS FROM THE DART AND FULLNESS

Yoke seams that pass close to the bust will not receive much fullness from the dart shape. They must have additional fullness added to achieve the desired design.

Notice that the fullness is distributed into the pattern by changing both the waist and the armhole curve.

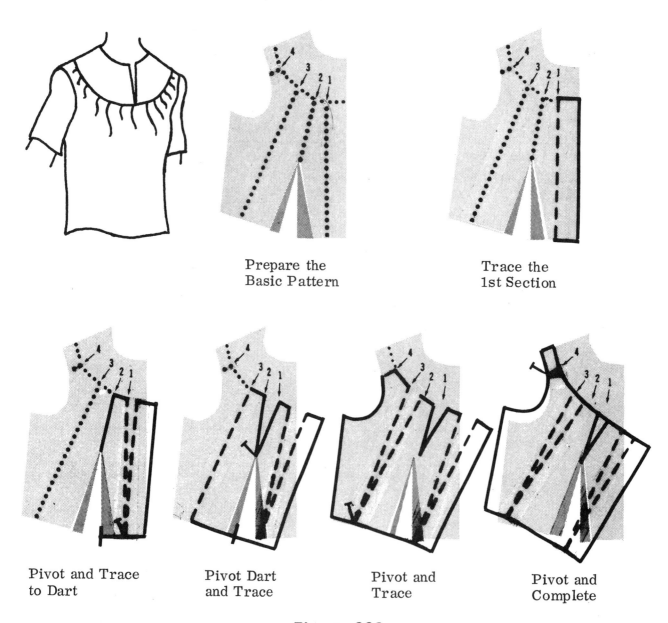

Prepare the
Basic Pattern

Trace the
1st Section

Pivot and Trace
to Dart

Pivot Dart
and Trace

Pivot and
Trace

Pivot and
Complete

Figure 228

YOKE VARIATIONS

Here are several designs for yokes that have
varying amounts of fullness added.

Figure 229

PLEATS

Pleats are a specialized type of fullness. The best procedure for creating patterns for pleats is as follows. Take a piece of tracing paper and fold it exactly the way the pleats are to appear. Transfer the shape of the pleated portion of the pattern to the folded paper. Add a 5/8" sewing allowance and cut the folded paper on this seam allowance line. Unfold the paper for the shape of the pattern. Mark the location of the folds clearly.

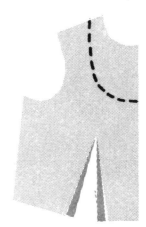

Prepare the Basic Pattern

BOX PLEATS

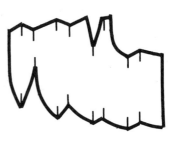

KNIFE PLEATS

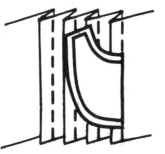

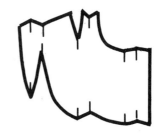

Fold the Paper

Transfer the Pattern

The Completed Pattern

Figure 230

SLEEVE VARIATIONS

Many different types of sleeves may be created by either changing the location of the seam lines, or by adding fullness to the patterns, or by using both techniques.

ADDING FULLNESS TO THE ARM SEAM

The sleeves in this illustration are created by changing the shape of the seam of the arm. The top of the sleeve remains fairly fitted. Fullness is added to the bottom of the sleeve.

A sleeve that is gathered at the wrist may have more fullness added to it in this manner than a loose sleeve. The gathers will keep the fullness evenly distributed around the arm. With a loose sleeve the fullness will tend to hang where it is added to the pattern, under the arm.

Important Note - To design the pattern for the gathered sleeve, expand the length of the pattern as well as the width. If a cuff is to be added, subtract the length of the cuff from the sleeve length.

GATHERED CUFF   LOOSE SLEEVE

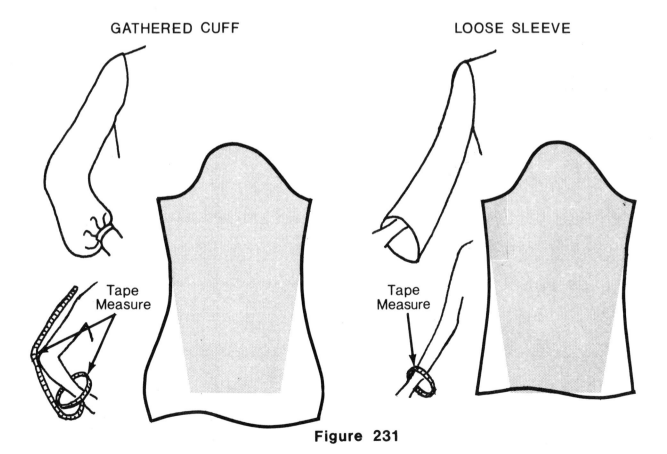

Figure 231

119

CHANGING THE ARM SEAM

Occasionally designs require very full, loose sleeves as in choir robes. If the fullness is added to the Arm Seam of the basic sleeve pattern, the sleeve will hang gracefully only when the arms are held out to the side of the body. When the arms are forward, the sleeve will twist. To prevent the sleeve from twisting, the Arm Seam must be changed to the back of the arm.

To change the location of the Arm Seam, mark the new seam on the Sleeve Cap. The back of the arm is halfway between the center of the sleeve and the side of the sleeve. Lay a piece of tracing paper over the basic pattern and trace the Sleeve Cap from the left side to the new seam location. Shift the tracing paper so that the traced left end of the Sleeve Cap touches the right end of the basic pattern. Trace to the new seam location. The fullness for the sleeve may now be added to the new seam.

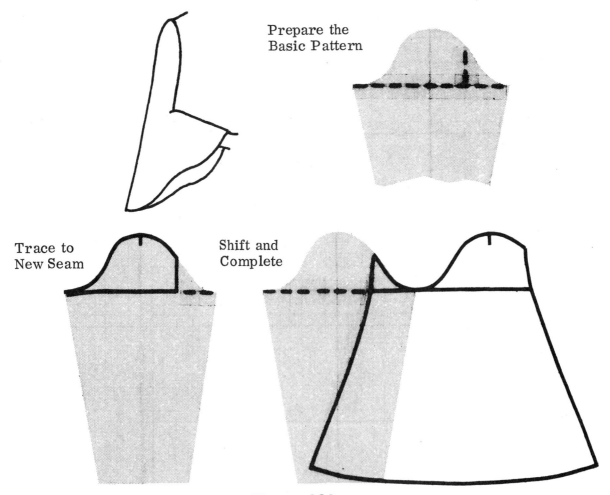

Prepare the Basic Pattern

Trace to New Seam

Shift and Complete

Figure 232

FLOUNCED SLEEVE

The design for Flounced Sleeves requires that the upper arm be fitted and the lower arm be full. To achieve this effect, a seam must be added where the sleeve makes a transition from fitted to full.

The upper portion of the new sleeve will be traced directly from the basic pattern. The lower portion may be created by adding dotted lines to the basic pattern where the fullness is to be added. Trace the pattern using the procedure for adding fullness to one seam (pages 108 and 109).

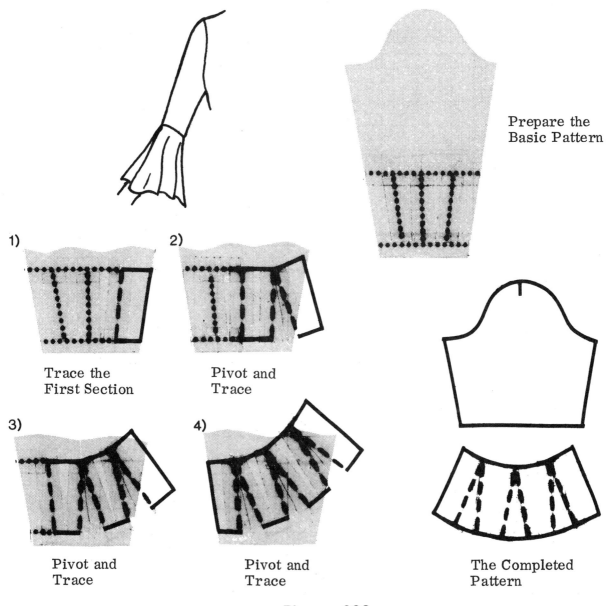

Prepare the
Basic Pattern

1)
Trace the
First Section

2)
Pivot and
Trace

3)
Pivot and
Trace

4)
Pivot and
Trace

The Completed
Pattern

Figure 233

GATHERED SLEEVE TOP

To create gathers in the Sleeve Cap, draw dotted lines on the basic sleeve pattern where the fullness is to be located. Trace the pattern adding the desired fullness.

If the arm portion of the sleeve is to remain fitted, pivot the tracing paper at the Biceps line. Add the bottom fitted portion of the sleeve as the last step. Notice that the height of the sleeve is increased as well as the length of the Sleeve Cap line being extended.

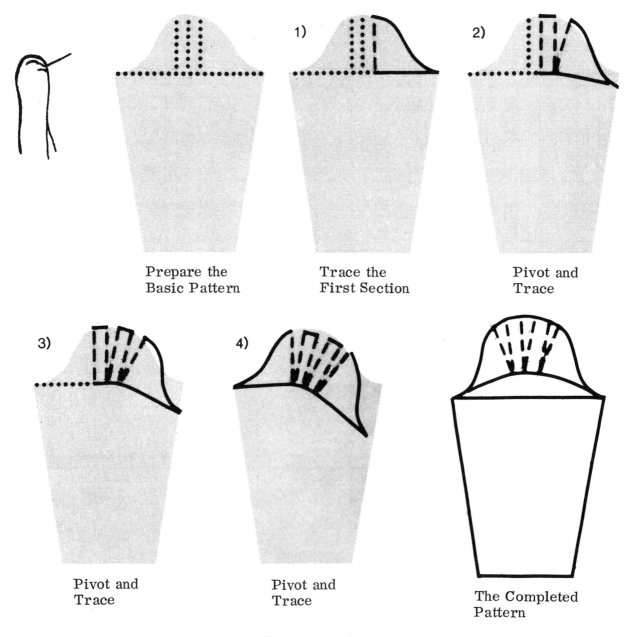

Prepare the
Basic Pattern

1) Trace the
First Section

2) Pivot and
Trace

3) Pivot and
Trace

4) Pivot and
Trace

The Completed
Pattern

Figure 234

GATHERED SLEEVE CAP

The fullness of the sleeve on page 122 will be
gathered into the top of the body of the garment. If
the fullness is to be gathered into more than just
the top, the pattern must be expanded across a
larger portion of the Sleeve Cap.

The dotted lines used to expand the Sleeve Cap
should be about one inch apart. They are set close
together in this manner because of the extreme curve
of the Sleeve Cap.

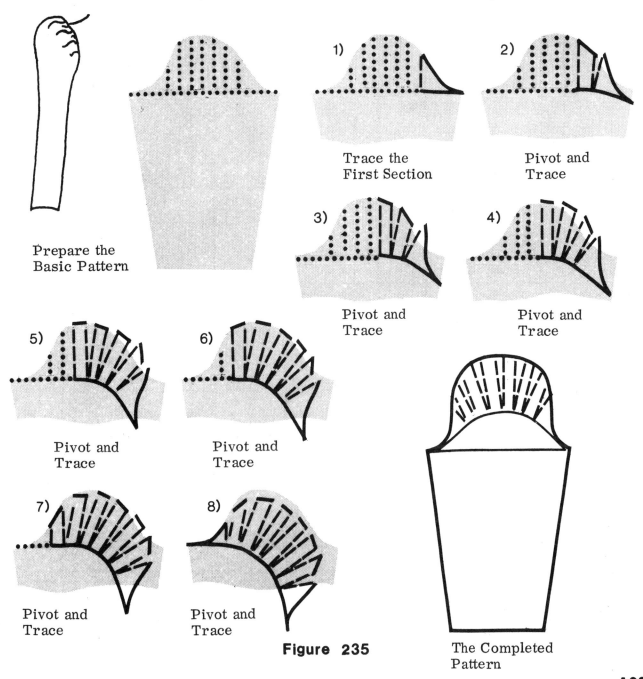

Prepare the
Basic Pattern

1) Trace the
First Section

2) Pivot and
Trace

3) Pivot and
Trace

4) Pivot and
Trace

5) Pivot and
Trace

6) Pivot and
Trace

7) Pivot and
Trace

8) Pivot and
Trace

Figure 235

The Completed
Pattern

LEG-OF-MUTTON SLEEVE

The Leg-of-Mutton sleeve has fullness in both the Sleeve Cap and the upper portion of the arm. The lower portion of the arm is fitted. Establish a line on the basic pattern to indicate how far down the fullness is to be located. Add dotted vertical lines to the pattern and place tracing paper over it. The tracing paper will be pivoted at the horizontal line that indicates the length of the fullness. Add the fitted portion of the lower arm as the last step.

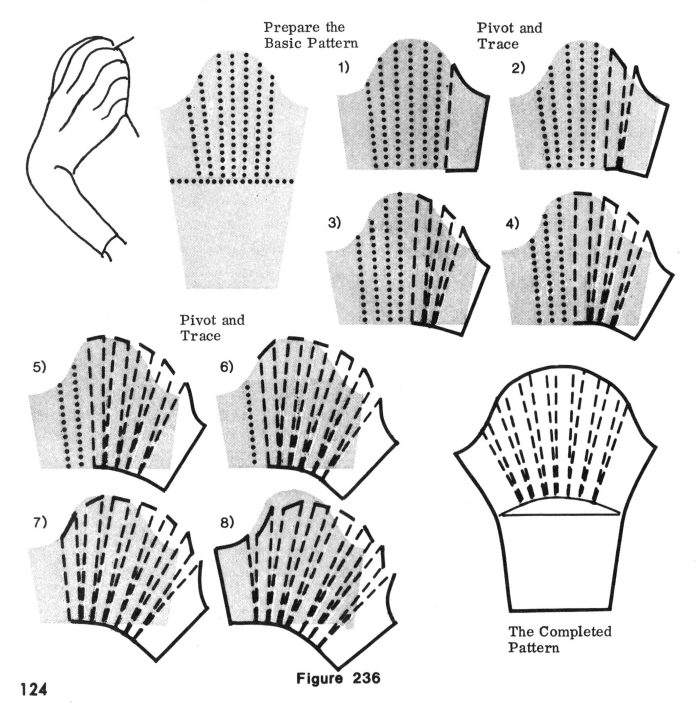

Prepare the Basic Pattern

Pivot and Trace

1) 2) 3) 4)

Pivot and Trace

5) 6) 7) 8)

The Completed Pattern

Figure 236

PUFFED SLEEVE

The Puffed Sleeve pattern has more fullness added to the top and the bottom seams than it has added to the width of the pattern. To achieve this effect, the pattern will be divided into an upper and lower portion at the Biceps line. The procedure for adding mixed fullness will be used (pages 112 to 114).

The Biceps line for both portions of the pattern will have a fourth again as much fullness added to it. The Sleeve Cap line and the Cuff line will have half again as much fullness added. The last step will be to combine the new upper portion of the pattern to the new lower portion.

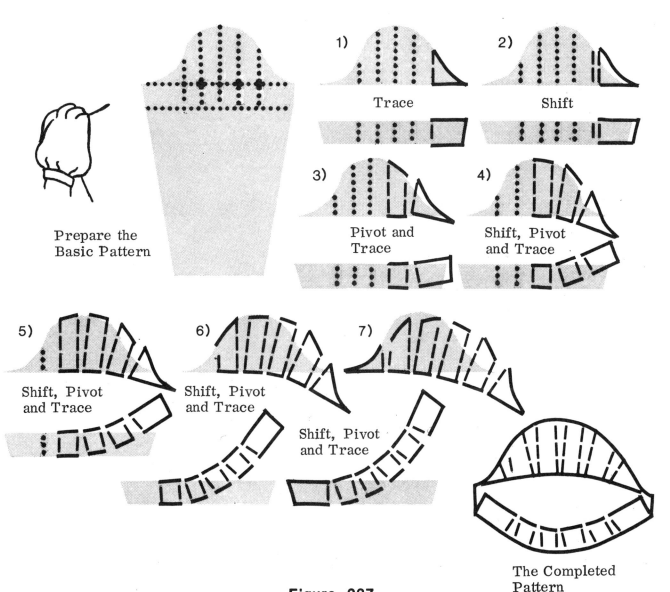

Prepare the
Basic Pattern

1) Trace

2) Shift

3) Pivot and Trace

4) Shift, Pivot and Trace

5) Shift, Pivot and Trace

6) Shift, Pivot and Trace

7) Shift, Pivot and Trace

The Completed Pattern

Figure 237

BELL SLEEVE

The design for the Bell Sleeve calls for the sleeve to hang away from the outside of the arm as well as the inside of the arm. To achieve this effect, the shape of the Sleeve Cap line must be changed.

Draw in dotted lines on the basic sleeve pattern where the fullness is to be added. Pivot the tracing paper at the Sleeve Cap line to add the desired amount of fullness to the bottom of the sleeve.

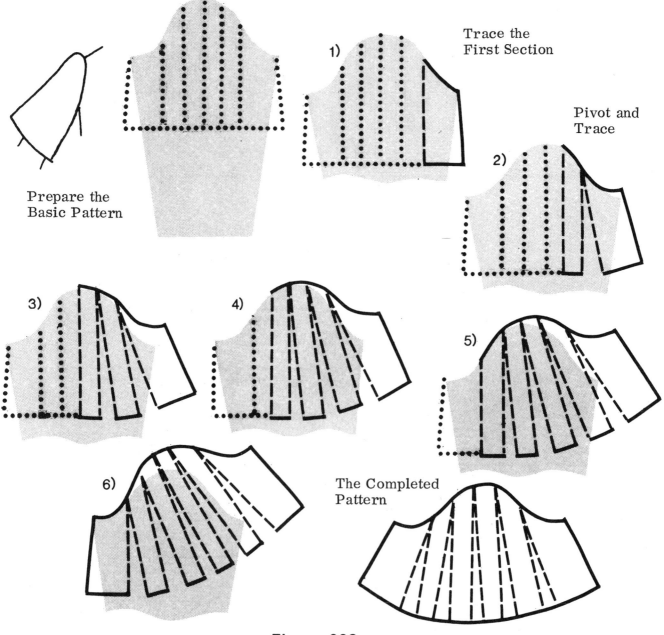

Prepare the Basic Pattern

1)

Trace the First Section

Pivot and Trace

2)

3)

4)

5)

6)

The Completed Pattern

Figure 238

CAPE SLEEVE

The Cape Sleeve is drafted the same way the Bell Sleeve is created except more fullness is added. There will be no gathers in the Sleeve Cap of this design.

To create this design, draw in the desired length of the sleeve on the basic sleeve pattern. Then draw dotted lines to indicate where the pattern is to be expanded. Pivot the pattern at the Sleeve Cap line to add the fullness to the Biceps line as is indicated by the measurements given below.

The extreme curve of the final Sleeve Cap line is what creates the draped effect of this sleeve. Notice that fullness has not been added under the arm.

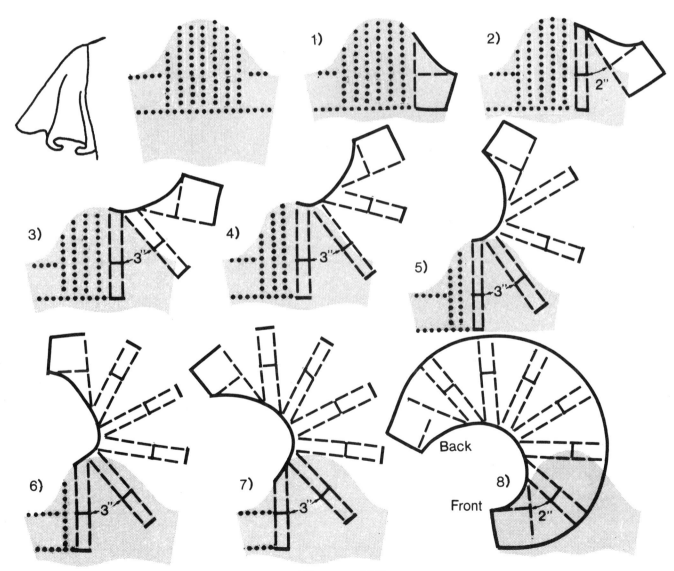

Figure 239

RAGLAN SLEEVE

The Raglan Sleeve follows the principle of changing the location of the seam lines. Draw in the desired shape of the Raglan Seam on the front and back basic patterns for the body of the garment. Indicate alignment notches.

Trace the sleeve pattern. Place the Shoulder Point of the traced sleeve pattern on top of the Shoulder Point of the front basic pattern. Put a pin through both patterns at this point. Pivot the traced sleeve pattern until the Sleeve Cap line touches the Armhole Curve at the new Raglan Seam line. Trace the upper portion of the Raglan Sleeve from the basic front pattern.

Follow the same procedure for the back of the sleeve. The traced Shoulder Seams from the basic patterns form the dart of the Raglan Sleeve. This dart compensates for the shape of the body at the shoulder. The body bends in two directions at this point. One bend is from the shoulder down the arm and the other bend is from the front of the body to the back.

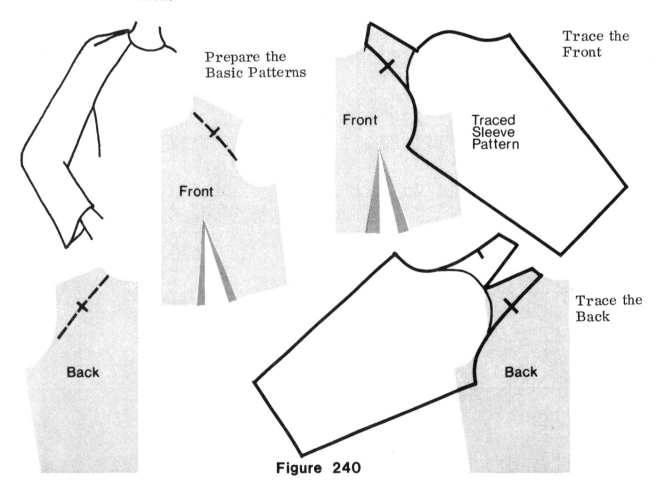

Prepare the Basic Patterns

Front

Back

Front

Traced Sleeve Pattern

Trace the Front

Back

Trace the Back

Figure 240

SQUARED SHOULDER SEAM

The same principle used to create the Raglan Sleeve may be applied to other designs. A portion of the body is added to the sleeve. However, the new seam lines on the body must intersect with the Armhole Curve before this curve goes under the arm.

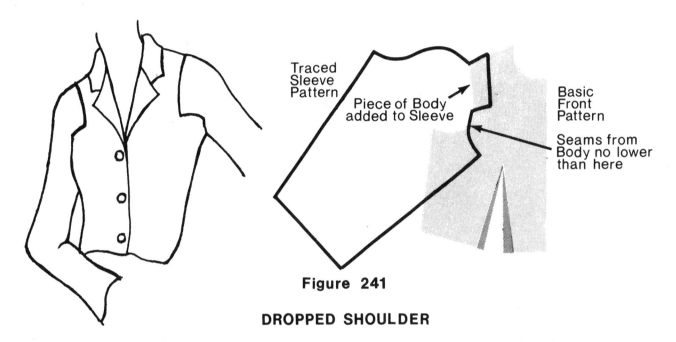

Figure 241

DROPPED SHOULDER

If a portion of the body may be added to the sleeve, then a portion of the sleeve may be added to the body. The Dropped Shoulder design is an example of this. This pattern may be used with or without a sleeve.

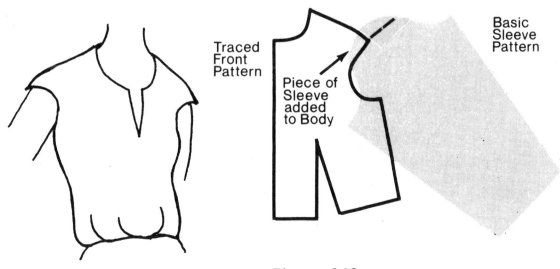

Figure 242

PEASANT SLEEVE

The Peasant Sleeve may be created by measuring the body directly according to the desired design.

Measure the Sleeve Top from the normal Shoulder Seam location to the desired top of the blouse. This measurement and the Blouse Top measurement will be doubled on the pattern to create double fullness. The Underarm Length should be measured up from the normal Side Seam location.

Fold the patterns along the Sleeve Top and the Blouse Top lines to create a casing for an elastic or a draw string.

The sleeves will be sewn to the body of the garment along the Underarm Seams. Sew the casing closed next. Then sew the Sleeve Seams and Side Seams.

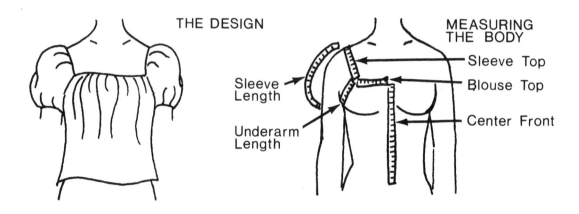

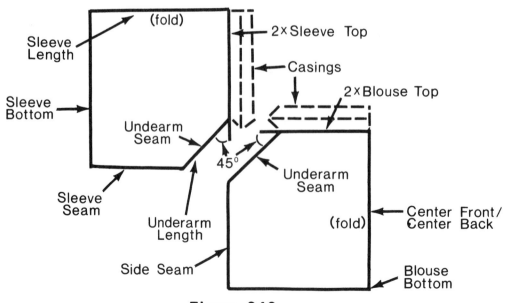

Figure 243

TUNIC SLEEVE

The Tunic Sleeve is historically the original sleeve pattern. The sleeve and the body of the garment are one continuous piece of fabric. This design is not meant to be fitted where the arm joins the body.

A common problem with this style is that the top tends to shift back making the fit around the neck uncomfortable. If this pattern is created from the basic patterns as described below this will not happen.

This design may or may not follow the slope of the shoulder. If the top seam does not follow the slope of the shoulder, there will be extra fullness at the top of the garment.

Seam lines may be added to this pattern in any manner. Seam lines may be added to simulate the Fitted Sleeve look or the Raglan Sleeve look. However, as long as the sleeve and the body of the garment lay flat on a table then it is a tunic sleeve. There is no shaping to fit under the arm in a tunic sleeve.

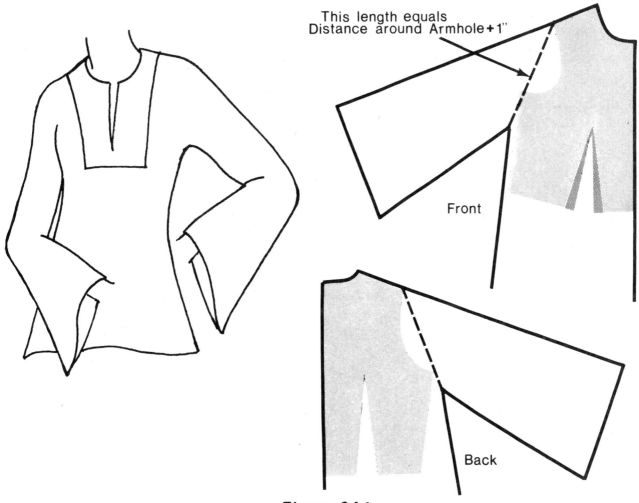

This length equals
Distance around Armhole + 1"

Front

Back

Figure 244

COLLARS AND NECKLINES

COLLAR STYLES

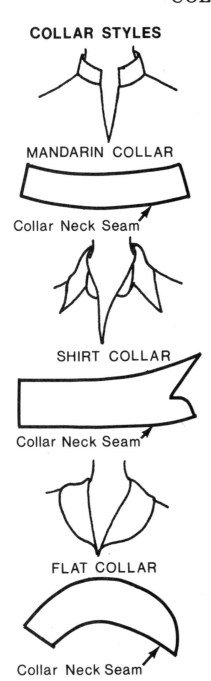

MANDARIN COLLAR

Collar Neck Seam

SHIRT COLLAR

Collar Neck Seam

FLAT COLLAR

Collar Neck Seam

Figure 245

Collars may be designed by the specialized pattern alteration techniques described here. There are three basic shapes that collars may take. The Mandarin Collar is shaped to follow the contours of the neck. The Shirt Collar follows the neck and then rolls over and falls back down. The Flat Collar follows the shape of the body instead of the shape of the neck.

The direction that the collar travels is controlled by the shape of the collar seam that joins the collar to the body of the garment. This seam will be referred to as the Collar Neck Seam. Figure 245 shows the three basic collar styles and the shapes of their respective Collar Neck Seams.

The first step in drafting collars is to determine the length of the Collar Neck Seam. Place the front and back basic bodice patterns together at the Shoulder Seam (Figure 246). Measure the distance from Center Front to the Center Back following the curve of the Neckline seam.

The length around the Neckline seam should be equal to half the Neck measurement (#1). Remember the Neck measurement was taken around the entire neck. If half of the Neck measurement is longer than the distance around the Neckline seam on the bodice, the Neck measurement may have been taken too loosely. If the length aroung the Neckline seam of the bodice is longer than half the Neck measurement, then the Neck measurement may have been taken too tight, or the Neckline of the fitted bodice may have been drawn too far out from the neck. Check the dimensions carefully. The corrected length will be referred to as the Neck measurement.

NECK SEAM LENGTH

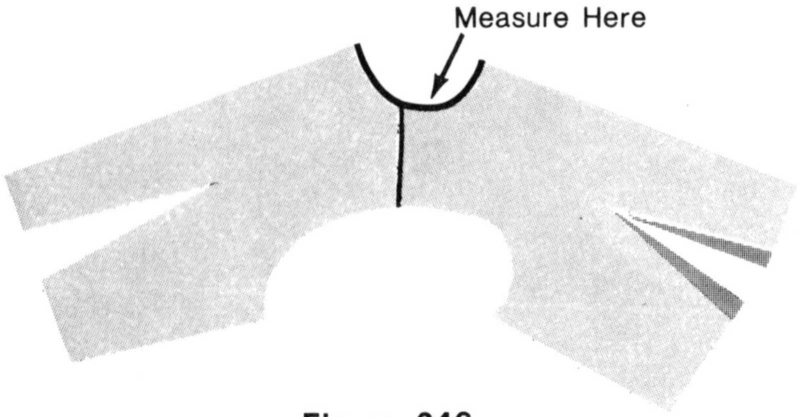

Measure Here

Figure 246

The Mandarin Collar

THE COLLAR SIZE

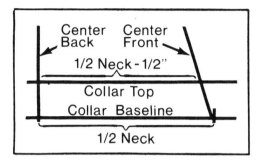

Figure 247

The Mandarin Collar is designed to follow the shape of the neck. Notice how the neck tapers from large to small as the neck gets closer to the head (Figure 245). The Mandarin Collar must, therefore, taper from a long Collar Neck Seam to a shorter Collar Top seam. These two seams must then be curved to keep them following the taper of the neck evenly around the body.

The procedure used to curve the Collar Top Seam and the Collar Neck Seam may also be used to curve the seam lines of other patterns as well. This technique for curving seams may be used to shape full skirts, for instance, and long tapered cuffs on sleeves.

THE COLLAR DIMENSIONS

Step 1. At a distance of one inch in from the left hand edge of a piece of $8\frac{1}{2}$" x 11" paper, draw a vertical line. This is the Center Back Fold line (Figure 247).

Step 2. At a distance of two inches from the bottom of the paper, draw a line at right angles to the Center Back Fold line. This will be the Collar Baseline. Extend the Collar Baseline a half an inch to the left of the Center Back Fold line.

Step 3. Mark off one-half the Neck measurement on the Collar Baseline starting from the Center Back Fold line and measuring to the right. This is the Center Front point.

Step 4. On the Center Back Fold line, measure up from the Collar Baseline the desired height of the collar. In this case the collar will be one and a half inches high. From this point, draw a line at right angles to the Center Back Fold line. This is the Collar Top line. Extend the Collar Top line a half an inch to the left of the Center Back Fold line.

Step 5. Subtract a half an inch from half the Neck measurement. Mark this length on the Collar Top line measuring out to the right from the Center Back Fold line. This is the Center Front point on the Collar Top line.

Step 6. Draw a line from the Center Front point on the Collar Baseline through the Center Front point on the Collar Top line. Extend this line about three inches above the Collar Top line.

These steps establish the basic size of the collar. Now the collar seams must be curved.

CURVING THE COLLAR

Step 7. Turn the left hand edge of the paper pattern under at the Center Back Fold line.

Step 8. Now fold the pattern to the right so that the Center Back Fold line coincides with the Center Front line for its full length (Figure 248). Notice that this is a diagonal fold. Crease this fold.

Step 9. Keep the paper folded in this manner. The Collar Baseline and the Collar Top line, from the left side of the Center Back Fold, appear on the back flap of the paper. Mark these points from the Center Back Fold line onto the Center Front line.

Step 10. Without opening the folded paper, fold it a second time so that the crease on the left side will coincide with the Center Front line (Figure 249). Crease the new fold.

Step 11. Unfold the pattern. There should now be three creases in the pattern dividing the collar equally into fourths (Figure 250). Mark the creases with dotted lines and number them as illustrated.

Step 12. Fold the pattern back from left to right again. This time the Center Back Fold line will be placed on the first dotted line (Figure 251). Mark the points where the Collar Top and the Collar Baseline from the Center Back Fold line land on this dotted line.

Step 13. Move the pattern so that the Center Back Fold line coincides with the second dotted line (Figure 252). Mark the points from the Collar Top and the Collar Baseline at the Center Back Fold line onto the second dotted line.

Step 14. Move the pattern so that the Center Back Fold line coincides with the third dotted line (Figure 253). Mark the points from the Collar Top and the Collar Baseline at the Center Back Fold line onto the third dotted line.

Step 15. Unfold the pattern and connect the points on the dotted lines as illustrated in Figure 254. The lower curved line of this pattern is the Collar Neck Seam.

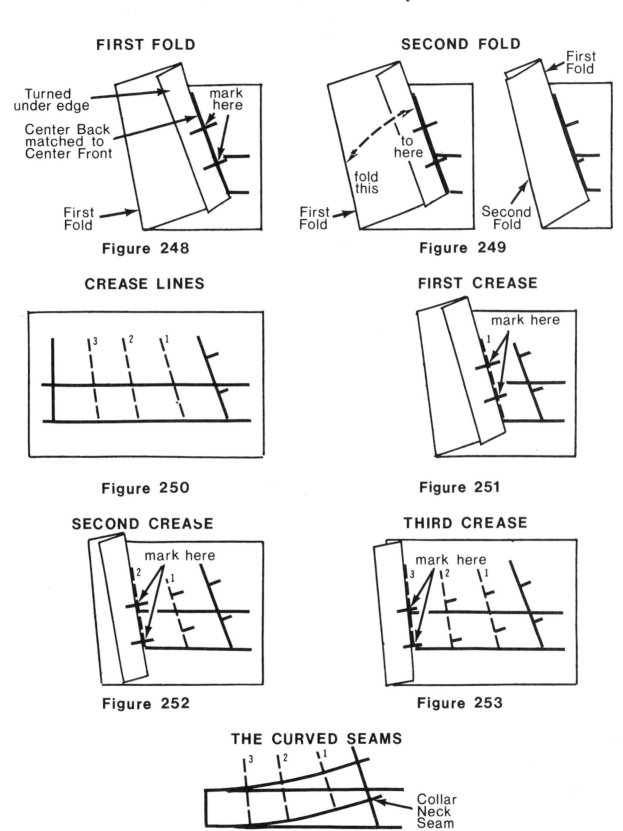

FIRST FOLD

Turned under edge

Center Back matched to Center Front

mark here

First Fold

Figure 248

SECOND FOLD

First Fold

fold this

to here

First Fold

Second Fold

Figure 249

CREASE LINES

Figure 250

FIRST CREASE

mark here

Figure 251

SECOND CREASE

mark here

Figure 252

THIRD CREASE

mark here

Figure 253

THE CURVED SEAMS

Collar Neck Seam

Figure 254

SHAPING THE FRONT

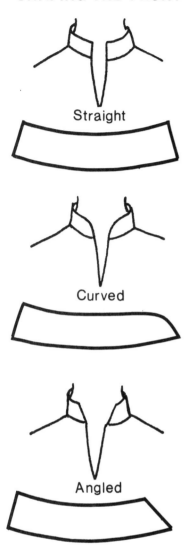

Figure 255

FINISHING THE PATTERN

Step 16. This procedure for curving the seam lines will shorten them slightly. To correct this, measure the straight Collar Baseline and extend the curved Collar Neck Seam to this length. Do the same with the Collar Top line.

Step 17. Connect the extended Collar Top line to the extended Collar Neck Seam to form the front of the collar.

Step 18. The front of the collar may be shaped to any desired design (Figure 255). These various designs will not affect the fit of the collar.

Step 19. Add five-eighths of an inch seam allowances to all seams except the Center Back Fold and cut the pattern out.

The Mandarin Collar illustrated here will follow the contour of the neck. To create a Mandarin Collar that stands out slightly from the neck, the pattern must not be curved quite as much. To achieve this effect, subtract one-fourth of an inch from the Neck measurement, instead of a half an inch, during Step 5. Figure 256 shows the difference between these two collars.

VARYING THE COLLAR FIT

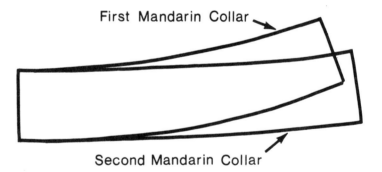

Figure 256

Shirt Collar I

THE BASIC SIZE

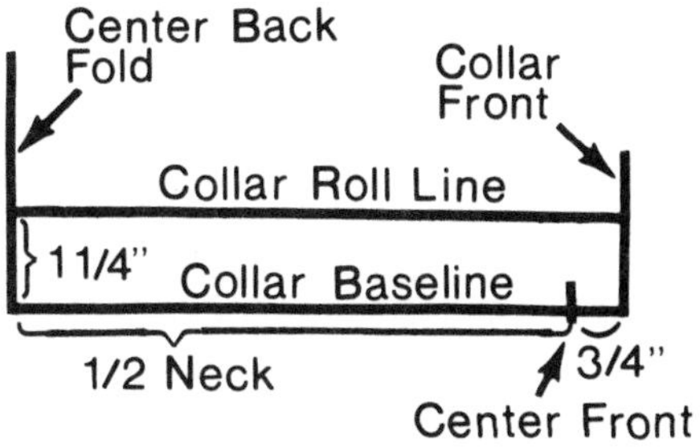

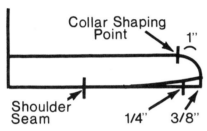

Figure 257

SHAPING THE BOTTOM

Figure 258

The Shirt Collar is most commonly used on men's shirts and some women's blouses. It stands up next to the neck then rolls over and falls away.

THE BASIC DIMENSIONS

Step 1. Draw a baseline for the collar. Mark off half of the Neck measurement (#1) on this line. This establishes the Center Back and the Center Front of the collar (Figure 257).

Step 2. At the Center Back point draw a line at right angles to the Collar Baseline. This is the Center Back Fold line.

Step 3. Mark a point three-quarters of an inch out from the Center Front mark. From this point draw a line at right angles to the Collar Baseline. This is the Collar Front.

The three-quarters of an inch added to the Center Front is for the button overlap of the shirt or blouse. Button overlaps will be discussed in more detail in the section on designing garments.

Step 4. On the Center Back Fold line measure up one and a quarter inches. From this point draw a line parallel to the Collar Baseline. This is the Collar Roll line.

The preceding steps have established the basic dimensions for the bottom of the collar.

SHAPING THE BOTTOM OF THE COLLAR

Step 5. Measure the Neckline seam of the back bodice from the Center Back to the Shoulder Seam. Mark this length on the Collar Baseline measuring out from the Center Back Fold line (Figure 258). This is the Shoulder Seam mark.

Step 6. Mark a point a quarter of an inch above the Collar Baseline at the Center Front mark.

Step 7. Mark a second point three-eighths of an inch above the Collar Baseline on the Collar Front line.

Step 8. Curve the Collar Neck Seam from the Shoulder Seam mark to the points established in Steps 6 and 7.

Step 9. On the Collar Roll line mark a point one inch in from the Collar Front. This is the Collar Shaping Point.

SHAPING THE TOP

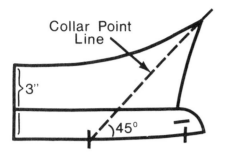

Collar Point Line

3"

45°

Figure 259

COLLAR SHAPING POINT

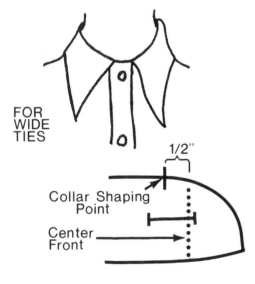

FOR WIDE TIES

1/2"

Collar Shaping Point

Center Front

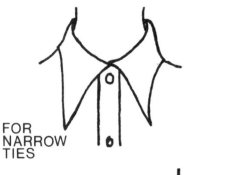

FOR NARROW TIES

Collar Shaping Point

Center Front

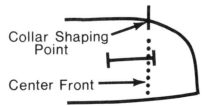

Figure 260

Step 10. Curve the front of the collar from the Collar Shaping Point to the Collar Front line. This curve is strictly for appearance and does not affect the fit of the garment.

Step 11. If a button is to be used, mark the buttonhole starting from the Center Front. The buttonhole should be half way between the Collar Roll line and the Collar Neck Seam.

SHAPING THE TOP OF THE COLLAR

Step 12. Draw a line from the Shoulder Seam mark at a forty-five degree angle to the Collar Baseline (Figure 259). This is the Collar Point line.

Step 13. Mark a point on the Center Back Fold line three inches above the Collar Baseline. This will be the top of the collar.

Step 14. Shape in the desired design for the top of the collar starting from the point established in Step 13.

The top of the collar should be kept parallel to the Collar Baseline until it passes the Shoulder Seam mark. If the collar is made too wide in this area, or if the top of the collar is not kept parallel to the bottom, the collar will not sit properly at the back of the neck.

Step 15. Shape in the desired front of the collar starting at the Collar Shaping Point.

For wide ties this Collar Shaping Point may need to be moved another quarter of an inch toward Center Back (Figure 260). For string ties this Collar Shaping Point may be moved to the Center Front line.

Sometimes the lower portion of this collar is separated from the upper portion so that extra stiffness may be added to the standing portion of the collar. To do this, cut the pattern along the Collar Roll line and add seam allowances to both sides.

This type of shirt collar is designed to be held close to the neck by being buttoned at Center Front. When it is left unbuttoned, it will spread to the side.

Shirt Collar II

SHIRT COLLAR FIT

Shirt Collar I

Shirt Collar II

Figure 261

THE STANDING PORTION

3/4" shift   Mandarin Collar

Figure 262

THE FALLING PORTION

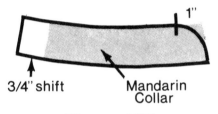

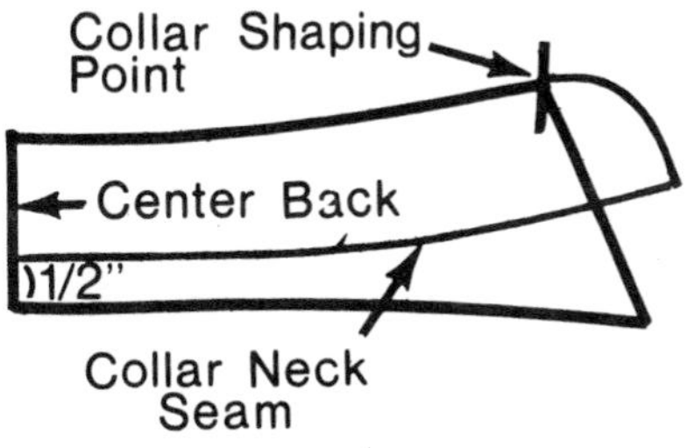

Collar Shaping Point

Center Back

1/2"

Collar Neck Seam

Figure 263

THE COMPLETED PATTERN

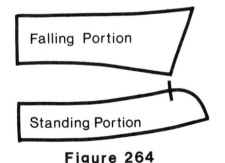

Falling Portion

Standing Portion

Figure 264

A second type of Shirt Collar may be designed to stand up closer to the neck even when left unbuttoned. This collar will be cut in two separate pieces. The lower piece will be based on the Mandarin Collar and the upper piece will fall down from this.

THE PROCEDURE

Step 1. Trace the Mandarin Collar from Center Back to Center Front. Shift the pattern to the side and add an additional three-quarters of an inch to the front of the pattern (Figure 262). This extra three-quarters of an inch is the button overlap.

Step 2. Measure in one inch from the Center Front to establish the Collar Shaping Point.

Step 3. Curve the front of the collar starting at the Collar Shaping Point. This completes the standing portion of this shirt collar.

Step 4. Place another piece of tracing paper over the Standing Portion of the collar.

Step 5. Trace the Center Back Fold line and extend it down a half an inch below the Collar Neck Seam (Figure 263).

Step 6. Trace the top of the pattern to the Collar Shaping Point.

Step 7. Draw in the desired shape of the collar. Usually a line drawn at right angles to the bottom of the Center Back Fold line will create a good collar shape.

Figure 264 shows the shapes of the two portions of this pattern.

The Flat Collar

THE FLAT COLLAR

Back

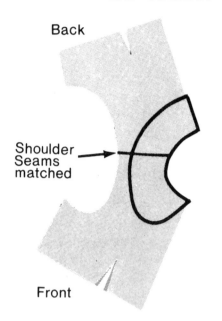

Shoulder
Seams
matched

Front

Figure 265

ROLLING THE COLLAR

Back

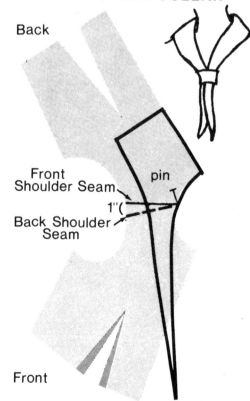

Front
Shoulder Seam

pin

1"(

Back Shoulder
Seam

Front

Figure 266

Flat Collars may be designed in many different ways once the initial shaping of the Collar Neck Seam is determined as described here.

The versatility of the Flat Collar is based on the fact that this collar is designed to shape to the body rather than the neck. Therefore, this collar may be used with any shape neckline and there is no restriction on shaping the backs of these collars.

THE BASIC FLAT COLLAR

The basic flat collar will be designed to lie perfectly flat on the body of the garment.

Step 1. Lay out the front and the back bodice patterns as if the Shoulder Seams were sewn together (Figure 265).

Step 2. Place a piece of tracing paper over the basic patterns and trace the Center Back line and the Neck Curve.

Step 3. Draw in the desired shape of the collar.

Step 4. Add seam allowances and cut out the pattern.

This pattern has a disadvantage in that the seam that joins the collar to the body of the garment will be exposed at the neckline. To eliminate this problem, the collar must be designed to roll up slightly on the neck.

ROLLING THE FLAT COLLAR

Step 1. Place the front and back basic bodice patterns together as before. Put a pin through both patterns where the Shoulder Seam meets the Neck Seam.

Step 2. Pivot the front pattern over the back pattern so that there is one inch between the Shoulder Points (Figure 266).

Step 3. Trace the Center Back and the Neck Curve as before and draw in the desired collar design.

The collar should be designed from the Collar Roll line indicated in Figure 266 because this is the exposed portion of the collar. The area between the Collar Roll line and the Collar Neck Seam will be the portion of the collar that rides up the neck.

Some designs may require that the flat collar stand higher next to the neck. To achieve this effect, increase the amount that the front Shoulder Seam is pivoted over the back.

LARGE PIVOTS

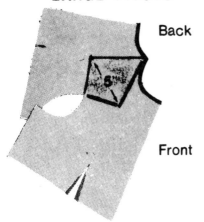

Figure 267

THE COLLAR NECK SEAM

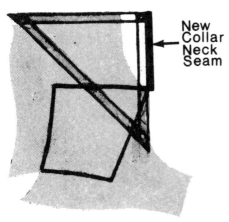

Figure 268

CHANGE CENTER BACK

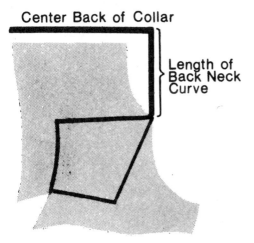

Figure 269

ADJUSTING THE FLAT COLLAR

If the patterns are pivoted at the Shoulder Seam so that there is more than two and a half inches between the Shoulder Points, the Neck Curve will no longer be a smooth line. Figure 267 shows the shape of the Neck Curve when the patterns are pivoted five inches.

To alter this neckline to a usable pattern the following procedure must be used.

Step 1. Pivot the basic bodice patterns as indicated and place a sheet of tracing paper over them.

Step 2. Place a right angle ruler on the Center Back line (the square corner of a piece of paper may be used).

Move the right angle ruler along the Center Back line until the other leg of the right angle touches the Neck Curve at the Shoulder Seam (Figure 268). Draw in a line along the edge of the ruler. This is the new Collar Neck Seam.

Step 3. Extend the new Collar Neck Seam further away from the Shoulder Seam with a straight line.

Step 4. Measure the bodice pattern from the Center Back to the Shoulder Seam following the Neck Curve. Mark this length on the new Collar Neck Seam measuring out from the Shoulder Seam (Figure 269). This establishes the new Center Back location.

Step 5. From the new Center Back mark draw a line at right angles to the new Collar Neck Seam. This is the Center Back line of the collar.

Step 6. Draw in the desired shape of the collar.

ROLL LINES

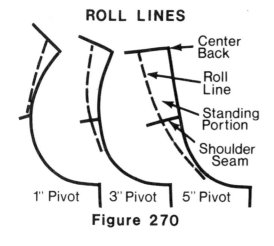

Figure 270

FLAT COLLAR CHART

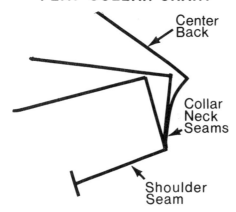

Figure 271

USING THE COLLAR CHART

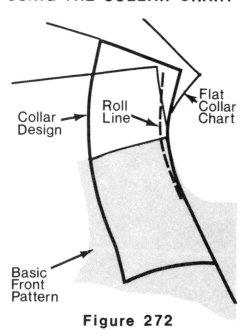

Figure 272

LOCATING THE ROLL LINE

The more patterns are pivoted at the Shoulder Seam, the more the collar will stand up next to the neck. The top of the standing portion of the collar should be indicated with a Roll Line.

Three different pivots of the Shoulder Seam and their respective Roll Lines are indicated in Figure 270. The approximate dimensions of these Roll Lines are as follows:

One Inch Pivot - The Center Back of the collar will stand up a quarter of an inch.

Three Inch Pivot - The Center Back of the collar will stand up three-quarters of an inch. At the Shoulder Seam the collar will stand up three-eighths of an inch.

Five Inch Pivot - The Center Back of the collar will stand up an inch and a quarter. At the Shoulder Seam the collar will stand up five-eighths of an inch.

THE FLAT COLLAR CHART

To create flat collars for a variety of designs, it is not necessary to pivot the patterns at the Shoulder Seam for each design. Rather, a composite of the various Collar Neck Seams and Center Back lines for different degrees of pivot may be combined into a single Flat Collar Chart. Figure 271 shows what this type of chart would look like.

To establish this type of chart, pivot the basic patterns so that there is an inch between the Shoulder Points. Lay a sheet of tracing paper on top of this and and trace the front Shoulder Seam, the back Neck Curve, and the Center Back line.

Pivot the basic patterns to three inches between Shoulder Points. Adjust the tracing paper so that the original tracing of the front Shoulder Seam still matches the basic front pattern. Trace the back Neck Curve and the Center Back line. Adjust the Collar Neck Seam for a smooth curve as was described earlier.

Pivot the basic patterns five inches. Match the original tracing of the front Shoulder Seam up with the front Shoulder Seam of the basic pattern and procede as before.

To use this type of chart, place the Flat Collar Chart so that the Shoulder Seam of the chart matches the Shoulder Seam of the front basic pattern. Draw in the desired neckline on the basic pattern. Place a sheet of tracing paper on top of the patterns. Trace the Collar Neck Seam and the Center Back line for the desired roll in the collar. Draw in the shape of the collar design.

Adding Fullness to Collars

Fullness may be added to collars by drawing the basic collar shape first. Then add dotted lines to this pattern where the fullness is to be added. Pivot and trace this pattern as was described in the pattern alteration section (pages 108 to 109).

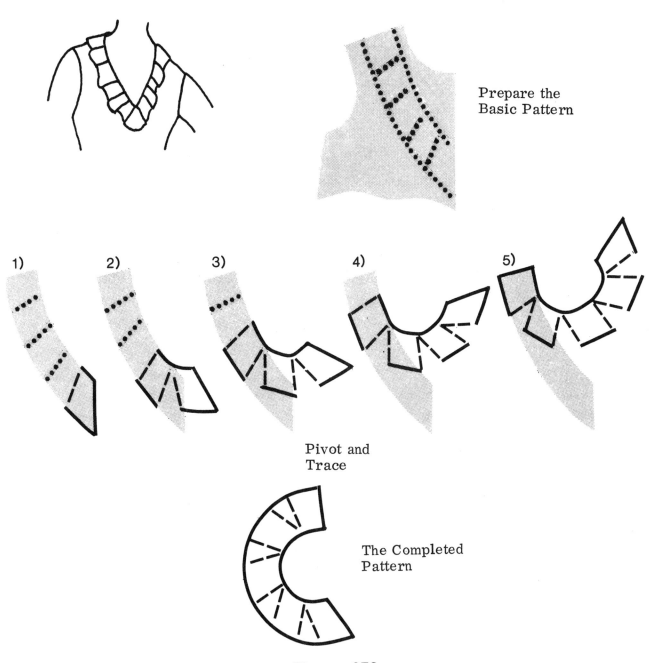

Prepare the Basic Pattern

1)   2)   3)   4)   5)

Pivot and Trace

The Completed Pattern

Figure 273

Cowl Necklines

DRAPE THE FABRIC

Figure 274

MEASURE THE DRAPE

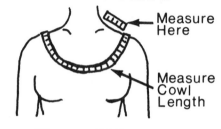

← Measure Here

Measure Cowl Length

Figure 275

MARK THE PATTERN

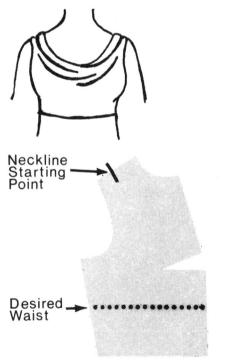

Neckline Starting Point →

Desired Waist → •••••••••••••

Figure 276

Cowl Necklines may be drafted by using the specialized pattern alteration technique described here.

Step 1.   Take the fabric that is to be used for the Cowl Neckline design and fold it on the true bias (this is a forty-five degree angle to the grain of the fabric). Hold it in the shape of the desired neckline (Figure 274).   See if it falls in graceful folds or breaks in unattractive creases.   Adjust the fabric for the best appearance.   Take note of the shape of the top of the neckline.

Step 2.   Recreate the desired shape of the neckline with a tape measure (Figure 275).   Determine how far out on the Shoulder Seam the Cowl is to start. Check the length of the draped neckline from one Shoulder Seam to the other.

Step 3.   Set up the front bodice pattern that has the dart to the Center Front line as the basic pattern (page 86).

Mark on the Shoulder Seam the point where the Cowl Neckline is to drape from (Figure 276).   This will be called the Neckline Starting Point.

Draw in a dotted line to indicate the Waistline. This Waistline may be established at any desired height.   A medium high waistline is illustrated here.

Place a sheet of tracing paper over the pattern.

Step 4.   Take a large right angle ruler (or a sheet of paper with a square corner).   Mark one of the sides as the Neckline.   Mark the other right angle side as the Center Front line (Figure 277).

SET UP THE RULER

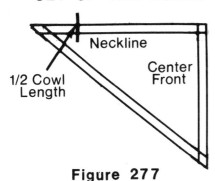

Figure 277

TRACE THE RULER

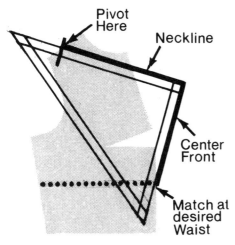

Figure 278

Step 5. On the Neckline edge of the ruler mark off half the length of the desired Cowl Neckline measuring out from the right angle. This is the Neckline Starting Point on the ruler.

Step 6. Match the Neckline Starting Point on the ruler to the Neckline Starting Point of the bodice. This will be the pivot point for the ruler.

Step 7. Pivot the ruler until the Center Front line on the ruler coincides with the Center Front on the bodice at the new Waist line as indicated by the dotted lines (Figure 278).

Step 8. Draw in the Neckline and the Center Front for the Cowl following the ruler edges.

Step 9. Trace the rest of the cowl pattern from the basic pattern (Figure 279).

The neckline of the cowl should not be a seam line. The pattern should be folded at the neckline and trace a facing that is two to three inches wide.

Figure 280 shows the completed Cowl Neckline pattern. A full front pattern with left and right sides is created for the cowl as this will be the easiest way to line this pattern up on the bias of the fabric.

For low Cowl Necklines, a fitted top should be designed to go underneath the cowl. This will eliminate any possible embarrassment when bending over.

TRACE THE PATTERN

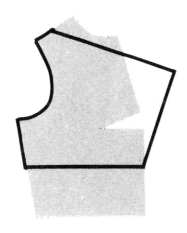

Figure 279

THE COMPLETED PATTERN

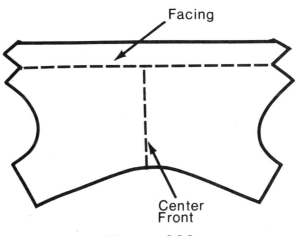

Figure 280

DESIGNING GARMENTS

Designing garments is primarily a matter of selection. The first step is to choose a body style. This includes determining the seam and dart locations, where the fullness is to be added, and how the fullness is to be controlled. The body style will be combined with an appropriate sleeve. Then a collar and/or neckline will be added.

The choice of the various elements should be co-ordinated through a sketch. This sketch can be made by drawing the clothing on top of a body silhouette. Body silhouettes such as those at the end of the book may be used, or the body silhouettes may be created by tracing photographs of the person who is to wear the garment. Tracing photographs will help to ensure that the proportions of the garment agree with the the proportions of the individual's figure.

After the basic shape of the garment has been determined, the design details must be established. The design details will include: how the garment is to be fastened whether it is with buttons, zippers, or a wrap around; the size, type, and location of the waistband; and the size, type, and location of the pockets.

The final design decisions will be how much ease to add to various parts of the body and the exact amount of fullness to give to the patterns.

SKIRTS

Skirts vary in design primarily by changing the amount of fullness and the manner by which this fullness is controlled.

The Fitted Skirt

The Fitted Skirt was described in detail on pages 25 to 32. It illustrates the closest possible fit in a skirt. All other skirt designs will have more ease and/or fullness added to the basic skirt pattern.

The Fitted Skirt did not have any ease added to the waist although a minimum amount of ease may have been added during the fitting. All skirt patterns must fit closely at the waist because the waist of the skirt actually rests on the larger part of the body just below the waist. If the waist of the skirt is enlarged, the skirt will slip down until it rests on a larger part of the body.

A Fitted Skirt design will usually have a zipper opening in either the Side Seam or the Center Back Seam. It does not need a Waistband unless one is desired because the shape of the garment will hold the skirt in place.

Full Skirts

THE BASIC PATTERN

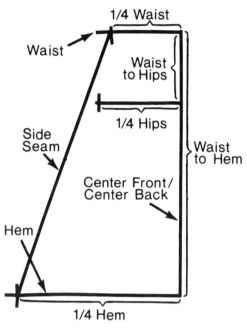

Figure 281

CURVING THE SKIRT

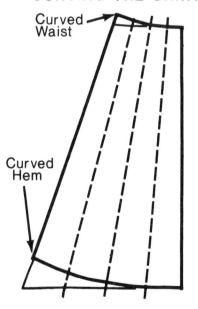

Figure 282

Full Skirts with fitted waists may be created by altering the fitted skirt patterns. This procedure will require closing out the darts and removing the shaping at the Side Seams as was described on pages 100 to 102. The Full Skirt may also be created by the following procedure.

THE FULL SKIRT PATTERN

Step 1. Draw a line that is the Waist to Hem length (Figure 281). This will be the Center Front/Center Back line.

Step 2. Draw a line at right angles to the top of the Center Front/Center Back line. This will be the Waist line.

Step 3. Determine how many sections the skirt is to have. These sections are called gores. The skirt may have four, six, or eight gores; or as many as desired. Divide the Waist measurement (#11) by the number of gores and mark this length on the Waist line. A four gore skirt is illustrated here.

Step 4. Draw a line at right angles to the bottom of the Center Front/Center Back line. This is the Hem line. Divide the desired Hem measurement by the number of gores in the skirt and mark this length on the Hem line. The procedure for estimating the desired Hem measurement is described on page 104. Connect the side of the Waist to the side of the Hem.

Step 5. Measure down the Center Front/Center Back line the Waist to Hip measurement (#35) and draw a line at right angles. This is the Hip line.

Step 6. Divide the Hip measurement (#15) by the number of gores and mark this length on the Hip line.

This step is a check on the pattern to make sure that the taper of the skirt from the Waist to the Hem has allowed enough room for the Hips. Adjust the Side Seam as necessary.

Step 7. Curve the skirt pattern using the technique described for curving the seams of the Mandarin Collar on pages 134 to 136 (Figure 282).

THE PLACKET PATTERN

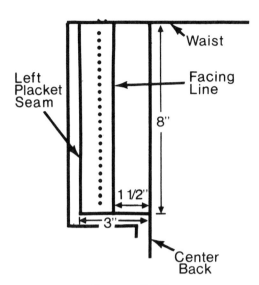

Figure 283

THE SKIRT PLACKET

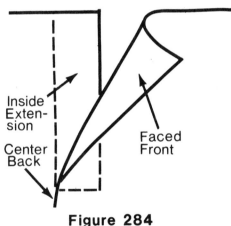

Figure 284

THE WAIST BAND

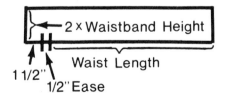

Figure 285

THE SKIRT PLACKET

A placket may be added to this skirt pattern at the Center Back. The placket creates an opening in the skirt that may be secured with snaps or buttons. The right side of the skirt will lap over an extended portion of the left side.

Step 8. Measure down the Center Back line eight inches and draw a line at right angles to it (Figure 283). This will be the bottom of the placket.

Step 9. Measure out on the bottom of the placket one and a half inches and draw a line parallel to the Center Back line. This is the Facing Line for the right, back skirt gore. Add a five-eighths of an inch seam allowance to this line by drawing a dotted line.

The placket of the right, back skirt gore will be folded at the Center Back line and top-stitched in place down the Facing Line.

Step 10. On the bottom of the placket measure out three inches and draw a line parallel to the Center Back line. This is the Left Placket Seam. Add a five-eighths inch seam allowance to it.

The Left Placket Seam on the left, back skirt gore will be folded so that it coincides with the Center Back line and top-stitched in place.

To cut the skirt out, cut the entire placket for the left, back skirt gore. For the right, back skirt gore, fold the placket pattern on the dotted line from Step 9 and cut the fabric here.

Figure 284 shows how the completed skirt placket will look.

THE SKIRT WAISTBAND

A Waistband is advisable to hold this type of skirt in place. Sew sturdy hooks and eyes into this Waistband.

Step 1. Add together the Waist measurement (#11), a half inch of ease, and one and a half inches for the placket overlap. Draw a horizontal line that is this length (Figure 285). This is the Waistband Seam.

Step 2. Draw lines at right angles to both ends of the Waistband Seam. Mark off twice the height of the desired Waistband on these lines. From these marks, draw a line that is parallel to the Waistband Seam.

Step 3. Add five-eighths of an inch seam allowance to the pattern and cut it out.

WRAP AROUND SKIRT

A Wrap Around Skirt may be created by making the full skirt pattern described above larger by one-fourth the Waist size and one-fourth the Hem size. This additional fourth will be the lap over portion of the skirt.

Leave the placket off this skirt. Make the Waistband at least three to four times the Waist measurement. this allows the Waistband to go around once with the skirt, a second time for the wrap around, and the remainder will be the tie of the skirt.

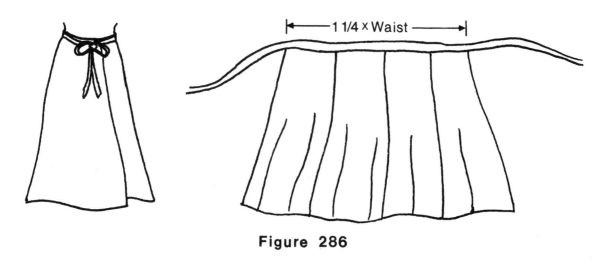

Figure 286

THE DIRNDL SKIRT

The Dirndl Skirt is historically one of the earliest skirt patterns. It is a rectangular piece of fabric that is gathered at the waist (Figure 287). If this skirt is cut out of light weight fabric, the top edge may be turned over to form a casing for elastic.

The Pattern

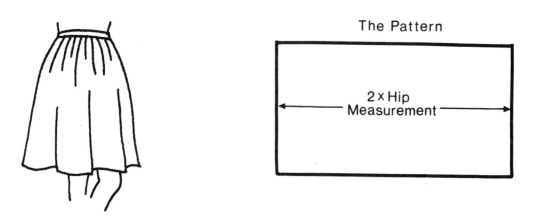

Figure 287

SKIRT VARIATIONS

Other variations of the skirt are shown here.
Pleated Skirts may be created by folding the paper as
was described on page 118. Ruffles may be added by
shaping the patterns as described on page 103.

Skirts may also be varied by changing the size of
the Waistband and by changing the opening from
zippers to buttons or the wrap around style.

Pockets will also add interest to skirt designs.
These will usually be patch pockets which will be
top-stitched in place. They may be designed to any
shape desired.

Figure 288

PANTS

Variations in the styling of pants were given on pages 43 and 44. The remaining considerations in designing pants patterns will be how to create waistbands, plackets, pockets, and cuffs.

MEN'S WAISTBAND

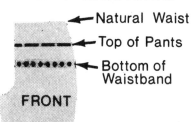

←— Natural Waist

←— Top of Pants

←— Bottom of Waistband

FRONT

BACK

Figure 289

WOMEN'S WAISTBAND

Bottom of Waistband

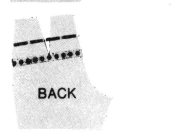

FRONT   BACK

Figure 290

HIP HUGGERS

Ease

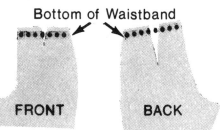

FRONT   BACK

Figure 291

Waistbands

There are two basic types of waistbands: the Straight Waistband and the Contoured Waistband.

The first step in designing either waistband is to determine the height of the pants pattern and the width of the waistband.

For Men - Men's pants are usually not cut to the natural waist (the height of the navel). They are two to three inches lower than this. The correct height for the pants should have been determined during the fitting (page 42, Step 9).

The pants pattern must now be lowered by the width of the waistband (Figure 289). This distance should be the same as the width of the belt that is to be worn with the pants, but not less than one inch wide.

For Women - The tops of women's pants are usually at the natural waist. This height was determined during the fitting. A waistband at this point will normally be about one inch wide. The middle of the waistband should coincide with the top of the fitted pants pattern. Therefore, the pants pattern must be dropped by half the waistband width, a half an inch in this case (Figure 290).

Pants may also be styled lower on the body as in the Hip Hugger pants. To achieve this design, determine the desired height of the pants during a fitting. Subtract the width of the waistband to get the correct height for the pants pattern. Remove the ease at the Side Seams for the waistband (Figure 291).

For Men and Women - To determine the length of the waistband, measure the pants pattern at the new seam line that will join the pants to the waistband. Measure this distance from Center Front to Center Back. Multiply this length by two to get the distance around the entire body. This will be referred to as the Waistband Length.

STRAIGHT WAISTBAND

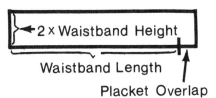

Figure 292

PREPARE THE BASIC

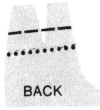

Natural Waist

Top of Pants

Bottom of Waistband

FRONT

BACK

Figure 293

TRACE CENTER BACK

Top of Pants

Bottom of Waistband

Trace to Dart

BACK

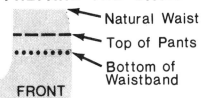

Figure 294

TRACE SIDE BACK

Shift to Here

Back Side Seam

Trace

BACK

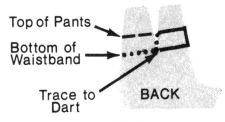

Figure 295

THE STRAIGHT WAISTBAND

Step 1. Draw a line and mark off the Waistband Length. Add the width of the placket at one end of this line. This will usually be one and a half inches (Figure 292). This line is the Waistband Seam.

Step 2. Draw lines at right angles to both ends of the Waistband Seam. Mark off twice the height of the desired waistband of these lines. From these marks draw a line that is parallel to the Waistband Seam.

Step 3. Add five-eighths of an inch seam allowance to the pattern and cut it out.

THE CONTOURED WAISTBAND

The Contoured Waistband is designed to follow the shape of the body. The description below shows how to create a Contoured Waistband for men's pants. The same procedure may be followed to create a Contoured Waistband for women.

Step 1. Draw in the desired top for the pants on the basic pattern. Then draw in the width of the waistband (Figure 293).

Step 2. Place a piece of tracing paper over the basic patterns and trace from the Center Back to the Hip Dart (Figure 294). Draw a dotted line to indicate the closest leg of the Hip Dart.

Step 3. Shift the tracing paper so that the dotted line coincides with the opposite leg of the Hip Dart (Figure 295). Trace to the Side Seam and draw in a dotted line at the Side Seam.

Step 4. Shift the tracing paper so that the dotted line from the back Side Seam coincides with the front Side Seam (Figure 296). Trace to the Center Front.

Step 5. Smooth out the curves of the Waistband and add seam allowances to all the patterns.

TRACE THE FRONT

Trace

Tracing from Back

Back Side Seam

FRONT

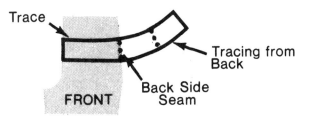

Figure 296

THE PLACKET

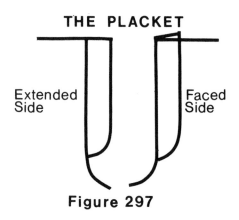

Extended Side

Faced Side

Figure 297

PLACKET DIMENSIONS

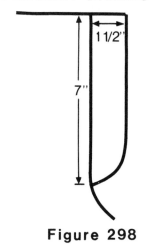

1 1/2"

7"

Figure 298

POCKET STYLES

Patch

Welt

Seam

Slash

Figure 299

Plackets

Plackets are a means of reinforcing garments where an opening is to occur. On one side the placket is a facing. On the other side, the placket extends behind the faced side (Figure 297).

For Men - The left side conventionally laps over the right side. Therefore, the left side is the faced side and the right side is the extension.

For Women - The right side laps over the left side. The right side is the faced side and the left side is extended.

Figure 298 shows the basic dimensions of the placket for pants.

Important Note - Do not extend the placket below the straight portion of the Center Front line. The garment is designed to curve under the body at this point.

Pockets

There are four basic types of pockets for pants: the Patch Pocket, the Welt Pocket, the Seam Pocket, and the Slashed Pocket (Figure 299).

The Patch Pocket is sewn to the outside of the garment. It may de drawn to any desired shape and top-stitched in place.

The Welt Pocket is created by cutting a slit into the fabric and sewing a pocket on the inside. This is an exercise in sewing rather than in drafting so it will not be described here.

If these two pockets are placed in the back of the pants, they should be kept on the side of the hip. This will prevent anything in the pockets from being sat on.

The Seam Pocket and the Slashed Pocket are created by changing the patterns so they will be described here.

THE POCKET SHAPE

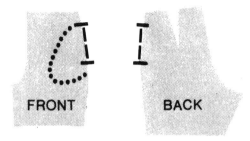

Figure 300

BACK PATTERN

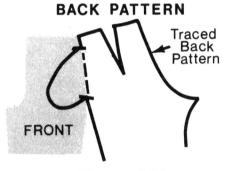

Traced Back Pattern

FRONT

Figure 301

SLASHED POCKET SHAPE

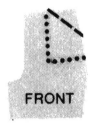

FRONT

Figure 302

THE PATTERN

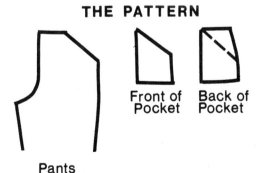

Front of Pocket   Back of Pocket

Pants Pattern

Figure 303

THE SEAM POCKET

Step 1. Determine the location of the desired pocket on the Side Seam of the front and the back pants pattern (Figure 300).

Step 2. Draw in the desired shape of the pocket with dotted lines on the front pattern. Trace this shape for the front part of the pocket.

Step 3. Place the back pants pattern so that its Side Seam coincides with the front pants Side Seam at the desired location of the pocket (Figure 301). Trace the shape of the pocket onto the back pattern.

Step 4. Add seam allowances to all patterns.

THE SLASHED POCKET

Step 1. Draw in the desired shape of the pocket opening on the front pattern by drawing dashes (Figure 302). Then draw in the shape of the inside of the pocket with a dotted line.

Step 2. Trace the pattern to get the three shapes indicated in Figure 303.

The exact shape of the pants are traced so that the pocket will not interfere with the hang of the pants. The pocket should be stitched to the Side Seam to keep it from shifting around.

Prefabricated linings for slashed pockets may be purchased from fabric stores in which case only the upper portions of the two pocket pieces will be used.

Cuffs

Cuffs may be added to any pants pattern. The following procedure may be used.

Step 1. Fold a piece of tracing paper in the desired shape of the cuff (Figure 304). The first fold establishes the inside of the cuff. The second fold is for the outside of the cuff. The third fold will be the hem inside the leg of the pants.

Step 2. Place the tracing paper over the pants pattern and trace the desired shape of the leg. Make the top of the cuff an eighth of an inch larger than the pants leg. This will keep the cuff from interfering with the fall of the fabric of the leg.

Step 3. Unfold the pattern and transfer all of the marks to the front side of the pattern.

THE CUFF PATTERN

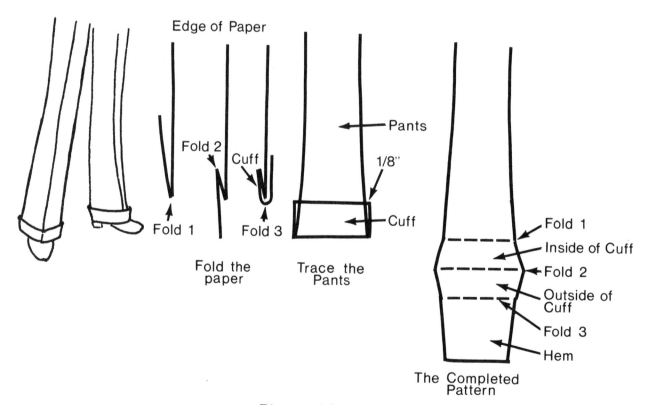

Figure 304

SHIRTS AND BLOUSES

Men's shirts are styled in a conventional fashion. This conventional shape will be described here. Many women's blouses are an imitation of this styling with the exception that a dart is usually added to the Side Seam. The location of this dart may be changed to create different designs.

The Body of the Shirt

The basic bodice patterns will be changed as follows to create the shirt pattern.

THE SHIRT LENGTH

Step 1. Extend the Center Front line down from the Waist line. Mark off the Waist to Hip length (#35) on this extension (Figure 306).

Step 2. Draw a line at right angles to the Center Front line from the Hip length. This will be the Hip line.

Step 3. Mark off one-fourth the Hip measurement (#15) on the Hip line.

THE SIDE SEAM

A total of two inches of ease will be added to the body dimensions on the front pattern to create a comfortable fit. Two inches will also be added for the back. This adds four inches to each side of the body for a total of eight inches of ease around the entire body.

Step 4. Add one inch of ease to the Side Seam at the Chest. Remember the basic pattern already has one inch of ease here.

Step 5. Add two inches of ease to the side of the Waist and the Hip marks.

Step 6. Draw in the new Side Seam using the ease marks described above as guides.

Step 7. Trace the Neck Curve, Shoulder Seam, and the Armhole Curve. Extend the Armhole Curve straight out to the new Side Seam.

This Side Seam may be styled in other ways also. For instance, a casual shirt that is designed to hang outside the pants may have a seam drawn straight down from the Chest to the Hip line.

THE TRADITIONAL SHIRT

Figure 305

THE BASIC SIZE

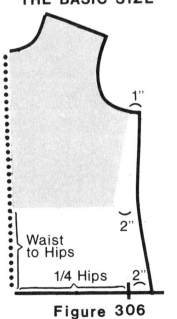

1"

2"

Waist to Hips

1/4 Hips   2"

Figure 306

SHAPING THE SHIRT BOTTOM

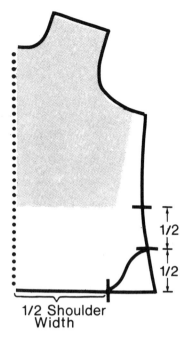

1/2

1/2

1/2 Shoulder
Width

Figure 307

SHIRT BUTTONS

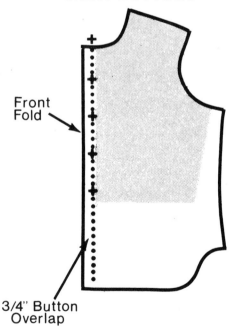

Front
Fold

3/4" Button
Overlap

Figure 308

SHAPING THE SHIRT BOTTOM

For shirts that are to be tucked into pants, the bottom of the shirt should be shaped on the side. This will prevent the shirt from riding up the side as the body moves.

Step 8. Mark off one-half the Shoulder Width (#3) on the Hip line (Figure 307). This measurement indicates the width of the front of the body.

Step 9. Divide the distance from the Waist to the Hips in half at the Side Seam.

Step 10. Draw in a curved line between these two points as is illustrated in Figure 307.

BUTTON LOCATION

Shirts are conventionally buttoned down the Center Front line of the body.

Step 11. Locate the first button one inch above the Waist line (Figure 308).

Step 12. The top button will be in the collar. Make a mark half an inch above the Neck line.

Step 13. Divide the distance between these two buttons in half for the middle button.

Step 14. Divide the distance between the bottom button and the middle button in half for another button.

Step 15. Divide the distance between the top button and the middle button in half for the last button.

BUTTON OVERLAP

The fabric for the shirt will have to extend beyond the Center Front to provide a means of fastening the buttons. This distance is normally three-quarters of an inch.

Step 16. Measure out three-quarters of an inch from the Center Front line and draw a line parallel to the Center Front line. This is the Front Fold of the shirt.

Buttons larger than three-quarters of an inch in diameter require a larger button overlap. The Button Overlap in this case should be the diameter of the button being used.

THE FACING

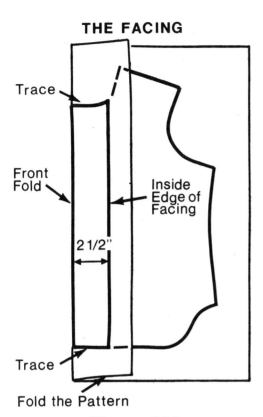

Figure 309

WOMEN'S BLOUSES

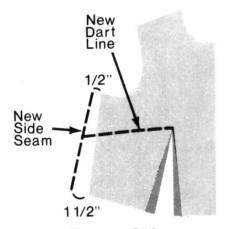

Figure 310

FRONT FACING

Step 17. Fold the pattern on the Front Fold line to create a facing (Figure 309).

Step 18. Trace the Neck Seam and the Hem of the shirt onto the facing.

Step 19. Measure two and a half inches in from the Front Fold line and draw a line parallel to it. This is the inside edge of the facing.

The facing is styled two and a half inches in on the garment so that the edge of the facing will not be exposed when the garment is left unbuttoned at the collar.

The straight edge of the facing should be placed on the selvedge of the fabric when the shirt is cut out.

THE BACK PATTERN

The back pattern may be styled the same way the front pattern was created except that the Center Back will be a fold line. When the Center Back is placed on the fold of the fabric and cut out, it will create a single piece for the back.

This completes the patterns for the body of the shirt. Other yokes and seam lines may be added to the basic shirt pattern by following the instructions on pages 80 and 81.

For Women - The same procedure may be followed to create blouses for women with two exceptions.

First, the Side Seam should be added to the basic patterns from the Armhole Curve to the Waist before the "A" Dart Shape is shifted to the Side Seam (Figure 310).

Second, six inches of total ease is usually sufficient for women's designs. This means that the Waist and the Hip should be extended out one and a half inches and the Chest should be expanded by half an inch.

The Shirt Sleeve

THE SHIRT SLEEVE

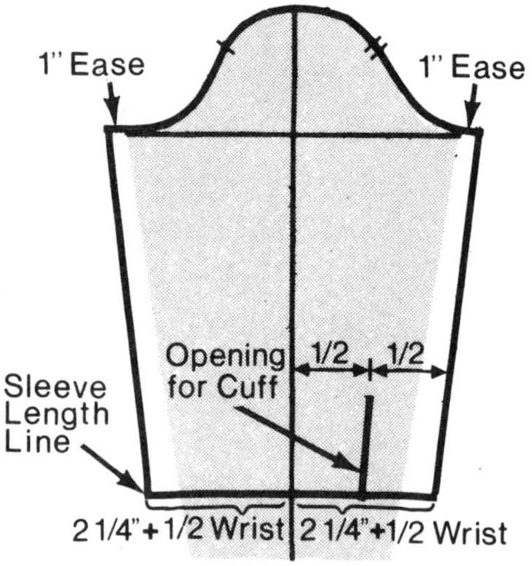

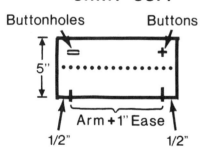

Men's shirt sleeves also have a traditional style.

THE SLEEVE

Step 1. On the basic sleeve pattern draw a line two and a half inches above the bottom of the sleeve (Figure 311). This is the Sleeve Length line.

The sleeve pattern must be shortened by the width of the cuff that is going to be added to the sleeve.

Step 2. Add two and a quarter inches to half the Wrist measurement (#13). Mark this length on the new Sleeve Length line measuring out from either side of the Sleeve Centerline.

This establishes the width of the bottom of the sleeve.

Step 3. Extend the Sleeve Cap line straight out by the same amount of ease that was added to the body of the design. This was one inch for men and a half an inch for women.

Step 4. Draw in the new Arm Seam from the expanded Sleeve Cap line to the new Sleeve Length line.

Step 5. The cuff of shirt sleeves open at the back of the arm instead of in the seam line. Draw a line for this opening that is half way between the Sleeve Centerline and the new Arm Seam. This line should be four to five inches long.

Figure 311

SHIRT CUFF

Figure 312

THE CUFF

A straight cuff may be drafted by the following procedure. A basic height for this cuff is two and a half inches.

Step 1. Measure the circumference of the arm two and a half inches above the wrist. Add one inch of ease to this dimension.

Step 2. Draw a horizontal line on a piece of paper and mark off the length determined in Step 1 (Figure 312). This is the Cuff Seam. The length of this line at this point is the distance from the button to the buttonhole.

FABRIC ALLOWANCE

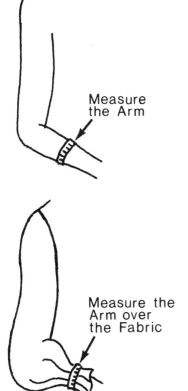

Measure
the Arm

Measure the
Arm over
the Fabric

Figure 313

Step 3.   Add a half an inch to either side of the Cuff Seam to create a Button Overlap.   Draw two lines at right angles to the Cuff Seam from these points.

Step 4.   Measure up five inches from the Cuff Seam and draw a line parallel to the Cuff Seam from this point.   Fold the pattern in half to determine the Wrist line of the Cuff (the dotted line).

Step 5.   Mark the location of the buttons and buttonholes on the pattern.   Add seam allowances and cut out the pattern.

The width of the cuff will be shorter than the width of the sleeve.   The difference between these two lengths will be taken up in pleats in the sleeve.   These pleats will be located on the outside portion of the arm.

Select an appropriate collar style from the section on collar variations.

Full Sleeves and Tapered Cuffs

Full sleeves and tapered cuffs present two additional considerations for pattern drafting.

FULL SLEEVES

A full sleeve will add additional fabric around the arm.   This additional fabric shrinks the effective size of cuffs.   To correct this problem, an additional Fabric Allowance must be added to the dimensions of the cuff when it is drafted.

Measure the bare arm at the desired height of the cuff (Figure 313).   Then measure the arm around the fullness of the fabric.   The difference between these two measurements is the Fabric Allowance.   This measurement may be as much as an inch or more depending on the amount of fullness and the weight of the fabric.

MEASURING FOR THE CUFF

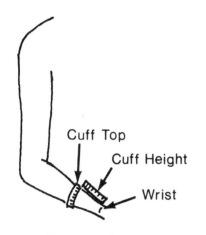

Figure 314

CUFF DIMENSIONS

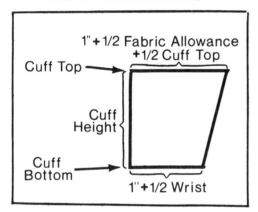

Figure 315

THE TAPERED CUFF

To draft a tapered cuff the following procedure may be used.

Step 1. Measure the arm where the top of the cuff is to be located. This is the Cuff Top Length. Measure the desired Cuff Height (Figure 314).

Step 2. On a piece of paper draw a vertical line that is the Cuff Height in length (Figure 315). Draw lines at right angles to both ends of this line. This establishes the Cuff Top and the Cuff Bottom.

Step 3. On the Cuff Bottom line mark off one inch plus one-half the Wrist measurement (#13). The cuff pattern must be drafted for half the cuff first. This will then be changed to a full cuff. The one inch added to the Wrist measurement adds a half an inch of ease and a half an inch of button overlap to the pattern.

Step 4. On the Cuff Top line mark off one inch plus half the Fabric Allowance plus half the Cuff Top Length (Step 1).

Step 5. Connect the mark on the Cuff Top line to the mark on the Cuff Bottom line to form the edge of the cuff.

Step 6. Follow the procedure for curving the seams described on pages 134 to 136.

Step 7. Fold the paper of this pattern along the Cuff Height line and trace the curved half of the pattern. When the paper is unfolded, it is the shape of the full cuff (Figure 316).

Step 8. Draw in the button and buttonhole locations a half an inch in from the edge of the pattern. Add seam allowances and cut out the pattern.

THE PATTERN

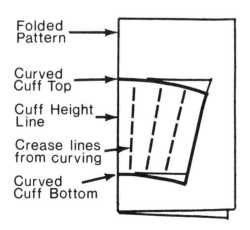

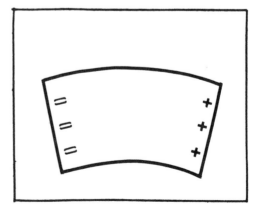

Figure 316

DRESSES AND TOPS

SHAPES OF THE BUST

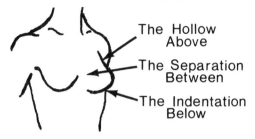

The Hollow Above

The Separation Between

The Indentation Below

Figure 317

MUSLIN FITTING

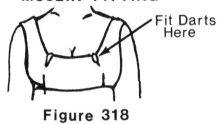

Fit Darts Here

Figure 318

TRACE THE FRONT

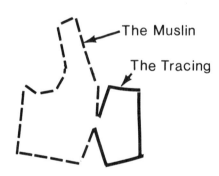

The Muslin

The Tracing

Figure 319

PIVOT AND COMPLETE

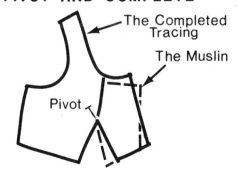

The Completed Tracing

The Muslin

Pivot

Figure 320

Dresses and Tops present an infinite variety of styling possiblities. Most of these designs may be created from the basic patterns using the alteration techniques already described.

The only designs which may require further modification are those which may pick up a contour of the bust that is not reflected in the basic patterns (Figure 317). The three shapes of the bust so involved would be the hollow above the bust, the shaping below the bust and the separation between the breasts.

Low Necklines

A Low Neckline cut from the basic pattern may not fit closely to the body because of the hollow above the bust. To correct this problem, fit a muslin top of the desired design.

Step 1. Put the muslin on and fit a dart into the neckline so that the fabric follows the body smoothly (Figure 318).

Step 2. Take this muslin off and mark the new neckline dart clearly. Remove the basting from the muslin.

Step 3. Place a sheet of tracing paper on top of the muslin. Trace the fitted muslin from the Center Front to the neckline dart and the designed bust dart (Figure 319).

Step 4. Pivot the tracing paper to remove the neckline dart. This will increase the size of the designed bust dart (Figure 320). Complete the tracing.

The lowered neckline has revealed the contour of the hollow above the bust. When fabric is shaped to this hollow, it must curve more than when it is shaped to the shoulder. Therefore, the size of the dart must be increased.

A low neckline in front must be accompanied by a high neckline in back. A low neckline in back must have a high neckline in front. This is necessary because the garment must be held up by the shoulders and shoulders slope. If there is a low neckline in both the front and the back, then the garment will slide right off the shoulders.

THE DESIGN

Figure 321

PREPARE THE BASIC

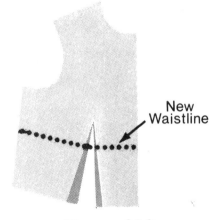

New
Waistline

Figure 322

High Waistlines

The High Waistline style is designed to fit closely under the bust (Figure 321). It may be created as follows.

Step 1. On the body measure down the Center Front to the desired height of the new high waistline. Mark this length on the basic front pattern.

Step 2. Draw in the desired shape of the new waistline. If the new waistline is to be parallel to the floor, as in this illustration, draw the new waistline parallel to the waistline of the basic pattern (Figure 322).

For curved and angled high waistline styles, measure down the body at the Side Seam from the armpit to the new waistline height. Mark this length on the Side Seam of the basic pattern and draw in the shape of the waistline.

Step 3. Place a piece of tracing paper over the basic bodice and trace from Center Front to the Inside Leg of the "A" Dart (Figure 323).

Step 4. Pivot the tracing paper to close out the "A" Dart Width and trace to the Side Seam (Figure 324).

TRACE THE FRONT PATTERN

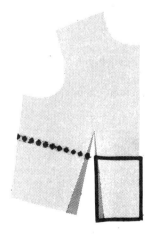

Figure 323

TRACE THE SIDE

Figure 324

SIDE FRONT TO RIB CAGE

Figure 325

THE TOP PATTERN

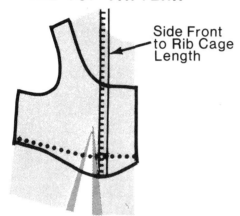

Side Front
to Rib Cage
Length

Figure 326

Step 5. Measure the Side Front to Rib Cage distance (Figure 325). Mark this length on the basic pattern.

Step 6. Place a piece of tracing paper over the basic patterns and trace the upper portion. Curve the waist line of the upper portion so that it drops down to the Side Front to Rib Cage length (Figure 326).

This curve on the upper pattern will appear as a straight waistline in the finished garment. The extra fabric will be shaped in under the bust.

If the dart shape is to be gathered, no additional adjustments need to be made to the pattern. If the garment is going to be fitted with a dart, the size of the dart will have to be increased in a fitting.

Wrap Around Closings

The Wrap Around closing for a dress or top may be created by drawing the desired design directly onto the basic patterns (Figure 327).

The Wrap Around Seam will fit between the breasts instead of riding over the top. The length of this seam must be shortened. Cut the desired design out of muslin for a trial fitting. Adjust the garment at the Shoulder Seam and at the Waist so that the grain of the fabric at the bust remains parallel to the floor.

THE WRAP AROUND

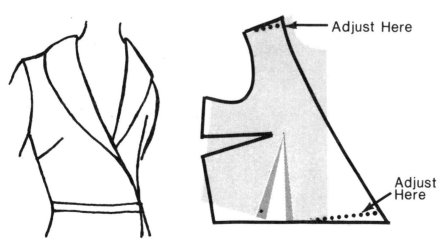

Adjust Here

Adjust
Here

Figure 327

JACKETS AND COATS

EXPANDING FOR JACKETS

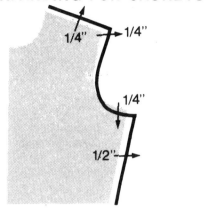

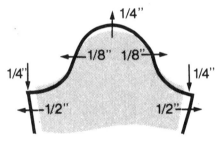

Figure 328

EXPANDING FOR COATS

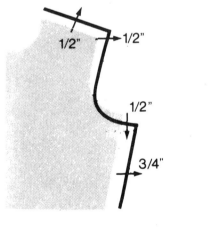

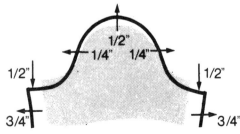

Figure 329

Jackets and Coats are traditionally the most carefully crafted garments in both styling and construction techniques. The patterns for these designs follow a few simple principles. Once these principles are understood, many different variations may be created.

Jackets, as described here, are garments which are worn over lightweight clothes such as shirts and blouses. Coats, on the other hand, are designed to be worn over Jackets and bulkier clothes like sweaters.

The fact that Jackets and Coats will be worn over other garments makes it necessary to first increase the size of the basic patterns. The seam and dart placements for the particular design may then be established on these enlarged basic patterns.

Another specialized aspect of shaping Jackets and Coats is the process of creating the lapels and collars. The lapel may be designed for either a single breasted or a double breasted style. The lapel may be shaped as a notched lapel, a peaked lapel, a shawl lapel and collar, or as a revers.

The final consideration will be to create the two piece tailored sleeve pattern.

Expanding the Basic Patterns

The basic patterns must be enlarged in order to style Jackets and Coats. The Shoulder Seam must be raised. The Armhole Curve must be made larger. And the Side Seam must be moved out.

The dimensions for increasing the basic patterns for Jackets are given in Figure 328. The dimensions for increasing the patterns for Coats are given in Figure 329. Expand the front and the back bodice patterns by the same amount.

Women's Coats and Jackets may be styled in many different ways from these enlarged basic patterns. Some of the possible styles are indicated in Figure 330. Men's Suit Jackets, on the other hand, have a traditional styling which will be described in detail in this section. The same principles may be applied to women's garments.

JACKETS AND COATS

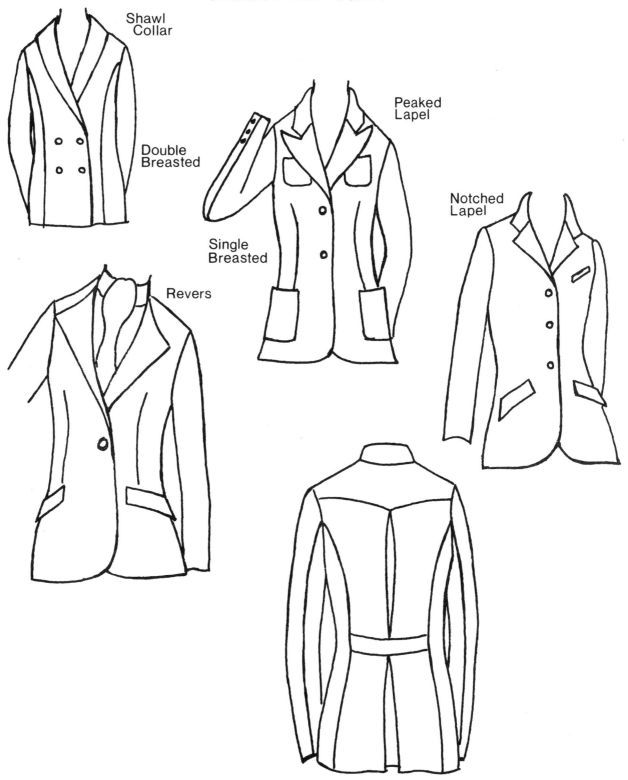

Shawl Collar

Double Breasted

Peaked Lapel

Single Breasted

Notched Lapel

Revers

Figure 330

PREPARE BASIC PATTERN

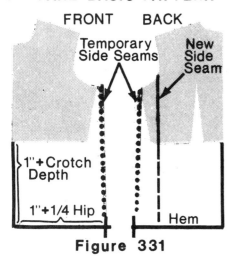

Figure 331

TRACE PATTERNS

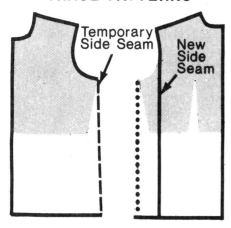

Figure 332

COMPLETE FRONT PATTERN

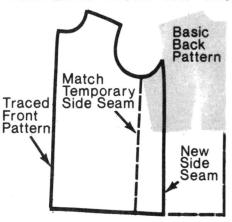

Figure 333

The Man's Suit Jacket

THE JACKET LENGTH

Suit Jackets are designed to hang down far enough to cover the torso portion of the pants. Only the leg portion of the pants will be seen below this jacket.

Step 1. On the basic pattern extend the Center Front line down below the Waist line. On this line mark off one inch plus the Crotch Depth measurement (#39). Draw a line at right angles to the Center Front from this point (Figure 331). This is the Hem line.

Step 2. On the basic back pattern extend the Center Back line down to one inch plus the Crotch Depth measurement below the Waist line. Draw in the back Hem line from this point.

THE SEAM LOCATION

The Side Seam on men's Suit Jackets is normally shifted to the back of the side.

Step 3. Add one inch to one-fourth the Hip measurement (#15). Mark this length on the back Hem line measuring out from Center Back. Mark this same length on the front Hem line measuring out from Center Front.

Step 4. On the front pattern draw a dotted line from the Armhole Curve to the mark on the Hem from Step 3. This is a Temporary Side Seam. Draw another Temporary Side Seam on the back.

Step 5. Find the point of the back Armhole Curve that is closest to the Center Back line. The new Side Seam will be drawn straight down from here parallel to the Center Back. Indicate the new Side Seam with dashes.

Step 6. Place a piece of tracing paper over the basic patterns and trace the back pattern to the new Side Seam.

Step 7. Trace the front pattern to the Temporary Side Seam. Indicate this line with dashes (Figure 332).

Step 8. Shift the tracing paper so that the Temporary Side Seam of the traced front pattern coincides with the Temporary Side Seam on the back pattern (Figure 333). Trace the back pattern to the new Side Seam line.

SUIT SHAPING

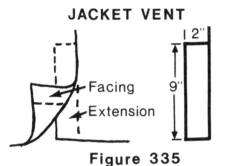

Figure 334

JACKET VENT

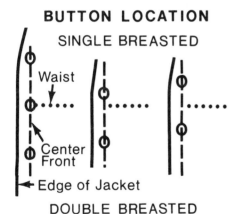

Facing

Extension

Figure 335

BUTTON LOCATION

SINGLE BREASTED

Waist

Center Front

Edge of Jacket

DOUBLE BREASTED

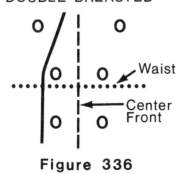

Waist

Center Front

Figure 336

SHAPING THE SEAMS AND DARTS

The shaping of the Suit Jacket is achieved by curving the Center Back seam, the Side Seam, and adding two darts to the front pattern. One of these darts will be at the old Side Seam location and the other will be directly below the man's nipple. This shaping should be done in a fitting.

The approximate size and location of these darts is illustrated in Figure 334.

THE JACKET VENT

A vent may be added either to the Center Back seam or to the new Side Seams. Figure 335 shows what this vent looks like.

One side of the vent is a facing and the other side is an extension behind the facing. This construction is similar to the plackets that were described earlier.

The dimensions of this vent should be about two inches wide and nine inches long.

BUTTON LOCATION

The button location of suit jackets is an important part of the styling of the garment. It will directly affect the shaping of the lapel.

Figure 336 shows the button location for traditionally styled garments. The spacing is listed below.

Three button single breasted - The middle button is at the waist, the top is four inches above and the bottom is four inches below the waist.

Two button single breasted - The top button may be either one or two inches above the waist. The bottom button is four inches below the top button.

Double breasted - The middle buttons are one inch above the waist and two inches to either side of Center Front. The bottom buttons are four inches below the middle buttons and two inches to either side of Center Front. The top buttons are four inches above the middle buttons and three and a half inches to either side of Center Front.

Step 9. Select the desired button location.

THE BUTTON OVERLAP

Buttons for men's Suit Jackets are normally three-quarters of an inch in diameter. The Button Overlap will be this same amount. If buttons larger than this are used, the Button Overlap should equal the diameter of the button.

Step 10. Measure out from Center Front the Button Overlap distance and draw a line parallel to the Center Front line.

LAPEL ROLL LINE

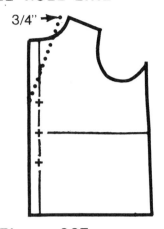

Figure 337

THE LAPEL SHAPE

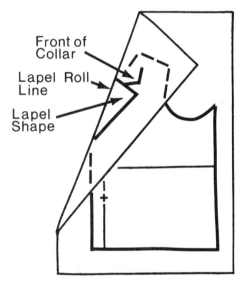

Figure 338

DOUBLE BREASTED JACKET

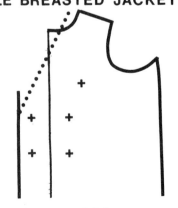

Figure 339

THE LAPEL ROLL LINE

Step 11. At the Shoulder Seam make a mark that is three-quarters of an inch in towards the neck (Figure 337).

Step 12. Make a second mark on the Button Overlap line that is directly opposite the top button that is to be buttoned.

In Double Breasted Jackets the top two buttons are not buttoned. They are only present for decoration.

Step 13. Connect these two marks to form the Lapel Roll line. This is indicated by the dotted line in Figure 337.

THE LAPEL SHAPE

Step 14. Fold the pattern on the Lapel Roll line and draw in the desired shape of the lapel.

A good reference point for the top of the lapel is the point where the Button Overlap intersects with the Neck Seam. The peak of peaked lapels may start from this point and the notch of notched lapels may be drawn from here.

Varying the lapel shape is one of the few changes that occurs in men's fashions. To achieve the current style, check the width of the desired lapel and where the lapel point is located on the body. Mark these measurements directly on the folded lapel pattern.

Step 15. Indicate the shape of the front of the collar as it relates to the lapel pattern. Unfold the pattern and transfer these lines to the front side of the paper.

THE DOUBLE BREASTED JACKET

A Double Breasted Jacket may be created by the same procedure. The main difference will be in the location of the buttons and the way in which this affects the Lapel Roll line. Figure 339 illustrates these changes.

SUIT COLLAR

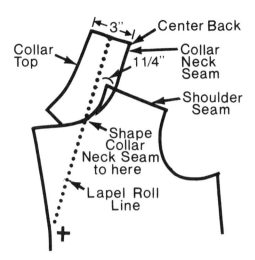

Figure 340

ROLLING THE LAPEL

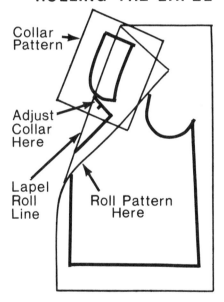

Figure 341

THE SUIT COLLAR

Step 16. Place a piece of tracing paper over the jacket pattern. Trace the Lapel Roll line and extend this line above the Shoulder Seam (Figure 340).

Step 17. Measure out from the Lapel Roll line one and a quarter inches and make a mark. From this mark draw a line that is parallel to the portion of the Lapel Roll line above the Shoulder Seam. This is the Collar Neck Seam.

Step 18. On the back jacket pattern measure the distance around the Neck Seam from Center Back to the Shoulder Seam.

Mark this length on the Collar Neck Seam measuring up from the Shoulder Seam. This mark is the Center Back of the collar.

Step 19. Draw a line at right angles to the Collar Neck Seam from the Center Back point to establish the Center Back line of the collar.

Step 20. Curve the Collar Neck Seam on the front part of the collar from the Shoulder Seam to the point where the Lapel Roll line crosses the front Neck Seam.

This completes the standing portion of the Suit Collar.

Step 21. On the Center Back line measure up three inches from the Collar Neck Seam. Draw a line parallel to the Collar Neck Seam from this point. This is the Collar Top.

Step 22. Draw in the desired shape of the front of the collar.

ROLLING THE LAPEL

The collar as it is designed here will hold the lapel flat to the body of the coat. A slight roll may be added to the lapel by the following procedure.

Step 1. Fold the front pattern on the Lapel Roll line. Place the completed collar pattern on top of this pattern matching the Lapel Roll lines.

Step 2. Hold the patterns carefully in place and shape the bottom of the lapel in the desired roll at the top button. This will cause the top of the lapel to pull slightly away from the collar pattern.

Step 3. Redraw the front of the collar to the lowered lapel top (Figure 341). This procedure must be done very carefully because as little as a sixteenth of an inch will make a difference in the shape of the lapel.

THE ROLL LINE

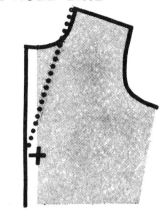

Figure 342

THE LAPEL

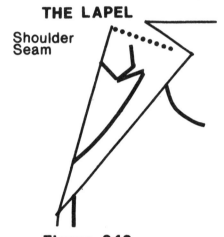

Figure 343

THE COLLAR

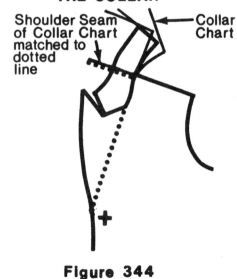

Figure 344

COLLAR VARIATIONS

Other collar variations may be achieved by using a Collar Chart like the one described on page 142.

Step 1. Draw in the Lapel Roll line from a point where the Shoulder Seam meets the Neck Seam to a point just opposite the top buttoned button (Figure 342). Notice that this Lapel Roll line is not shaped the same way the previous Lapel Roll line was shaped.

Step 2. Fold the pattern on the Lapel Roll line and draw in the desired shape of the lapel (Figure 343). Indicate the front of the collar. Draw a dotted line above the lapel where the Shoulder Seam is located.

Step 3. Unfold the pattern and match the Collar Chart to the front pattern at the dotted Shoulder Seam (Figure 344).

Step 4. Lay a sheet of tracing paper over the pattern and the Collar Chart. Trace the appropriate Collar Neck Seam from the chart for the desired roll of the collar. Trace the appropriate Center Back line. Draw in the desired shape of the collar.

REVERS

Revers are lapels minus the collar. They may be drafted by folding the pattern along the Revers Roll line. Then draw in the desired design (Figure 345).

THE TRENCH COAT REVERS AND COLLAR

The Trench Coat design is a Revers pattern with a Shirt Collar (I or II) shortened to stop at the top of the Revers Roll line. This allows the Revers to be either buttoned across the body or left open without changing the fit of the collar (Figure 346).

REVERS

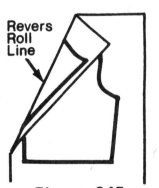

Figure 345

TRENCH COAT

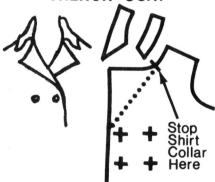

Figure 346

PREPARE THE BASIC

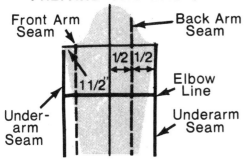

Figure 347

TRACE AND SHIFT

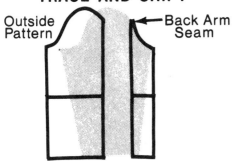

Figure 348

COMPLETE INSIDE PATTERN

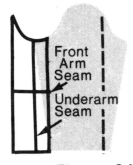

Figure 349

SHAPE THE PATTERNS

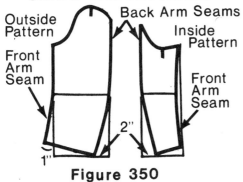

Figure 350

The Two Piece Sleeve

The sleeve on men's suits is conventionally shaped with a seam at the back of the arm and another seam approximately one and a half inches forward of the normal underarm seam position. The sleeve patterns are curved from the elbow to compensate for the angle of the arm as it hangs at the side of the body (see page 71).

Step 1. On the basic pattern redraw the Underarm Seams so that they are parallel to the Sleeve Centerline (Figure 347).

Step 2. Measure down the Sleeve Centerline the Shoulder to Elbow length (#33) and draw a line at right angles to the Sleeve Centerline. This is the Elbow line.

Step 3. Find a point on the Biceps line that is halfway between the Sleeve Centerline and the back Arm Seam of the sleeve. Draw a line of dashes from this point that is parallel to the Sleeve Centerline. This will be the new Back Arm Seam.

Step 4. Mark a point one and a half inches in from the front Arm Seam. Draw a line of dashes from this point that is parallel to the Sleeve Centerline. This will be the new Front Arm Seam.

Step 5. Lay a piece of tracing paper over the basic sleeve pattern and trace from the new Back Arm Seam to the new Front Arm Seam. This is the Outside Sleeve pattern.

Step 6. Shift the paper to the left to allow for seam allowances and trace from the Back Arm Seam to the right Underarm Seam (Figure 348).

Step 7. Shift the tracing paper so that the traced Underarm Seam from the right side of the basic pattern coincides with the left Underarm Seam of the basic pattern (Figure 349). Trace to the new Front Arm Seam. This is the Inside Sleeve pattern.

Step 8. Curve the Back Arm Seams of both patterns from the Elbow line to a point two inches in on the Wrist line. Draw new Wrist lines at right angles to the angled Back Arm Seams (Figure 350).

Step 9. Curve the Front Arm Seam of the Inside Sleeve pattern slightly as illustrated. Curve the Front Arm Seam of the Outside Sleeve Pattern from the Elbow line to one inch out on the new Wrist line.

Step 10. Measure the length of the Front Arm Seam on the Inside Sleeve pattern and adjust the Front Arm Seam of the Outside Sleeve pattern to the same length.

THE MUSLIN

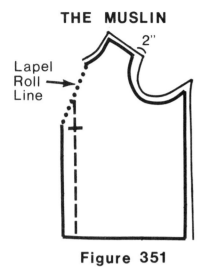

Lapel
Roll
Line

2"

Figure 351

FITTING THE MUSLIN

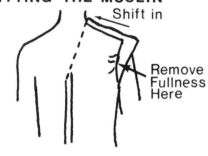

Shift in

Remove
Fullness
Here

Figure 352

CORRECTING THE PATTERN

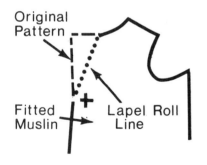

Original
Pattern

Fitted
Muslin

Lapel Roll
Line

Figure 353

Fitting the Man's Suit

The Suit Jacket may be fitted following the same procedures for fitting that have been used previously with the following exception.

Step 1. Cut out a muslin that is the shape of the front pattern up to the Lapel Roll line. Do not include the shape of the lapel. Add two inches of seam allowance to the top of the Armhole Curve (Figure 351).

Step 2. Place the muslin on the body in the normal manner at the Shoulder Seam.

Step 3. Now shift the Shoulder Seam in toward the Center Front of the body to remove any fullness in the muslin around the Armhole area (Figure 352). Correct the Armhole Curve and the Lapel Roll line to this new location. Remember that the Lapel Roll line should be three-quarters of an inch up the neck.

Step 4. Place the muslin on top of the original pattern aligning the new Lapel Roll line on the muslin to the Lapel Roll line of the pattern (Figure 353).

Step 5. Lay a piece of tracing paper on top of this and trace the muslin for the body and the original pattern for the lapel. This will be the pattern for the second fitting.

FACINGS

Facings are exact duplications of the seam lines that are to be faced. They should be taken from the patterns after all the fitting is completed.

Figure 354 illustrates a facing for the front of a man's suit coat.

FACINGS

Figure 354

FABRIC

There are a large variety of fabrics available for clothing construction. Each fabric has specific qualities which establish its character. Some of these qualities, such as color and texture, affect the appearance of the garment but not the fit. Other qualities, such as drape, flexibility, and weight must be taken into consideration during the drafting process. If these qualities are ignored, they can mar the effectiveness of the finished garment.

Understanding the drape, flexibility, and weight of a material is primarily a matter of developing a sensitive touch. There are too many different types of material and too many end uses for each type to make any kind of specific measurement a practical consideration. The material must be aesthetically judged rather than scientifically measured.

FABRIC QUALITIES

The pattern drafter must learn how to respond to each new piece of material as though it had a personality of its own. Two different materials will respond differently to the same pattern and the pattern drafter must learn how to design the patterns accordingly. Once again, time and experience are the best way to learn how to handle fabrics, but it helps to know what qualities to look for.

TESTING DRAPE

Drape on the Bias

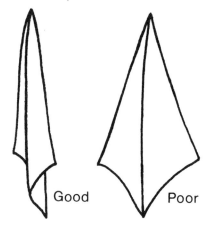

Good   Poor

Drape on the Straight

Good   Poor

Figure 355

TESTING FLEXIBILITY

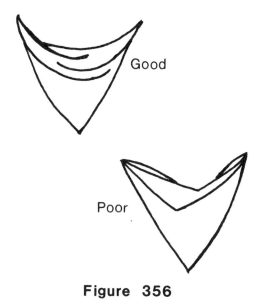

Good

Poor

Figure 356

Drape

Drape is the ability of a fabric to fall into even and graceful folds when it is left free to hang. Any design which requires part of a garment to hang from gathered seams should be made from material that drapes well.

A basic procedure for determining how well a fabric will drape is to pick up a corner and let the material hang on the bias. Check to see how easily the material falls into folds. Are the folds deep and do they pick up light to accent the drape? Notice any tendency toward stiffness (Figure 355).

Normally, a fabric's ability to drape may be determined by letting it hang on the bias. However, some materials will drape well on the bias but poorly when hung on the straight of the grain. To check for this quality, gather the top of the material into large pleats or gathers and note whether the material tends to fight the gathers, or whether it falls into graceful folds.

Generally speaking, tightly woven fabrics or fabrics using tightly spun yarns will not drape as well as fabrics that are either loosely woven or loosely spun or both. Knits tend to drape well because of the looseness of their construction.

Consideration should also be given to cutting the patterns on the bias of the fabric for collars, ruffles, and sleeves that are to have a soft look. In the 1930's whole dresses would be cut on the bias to obtain a softly draped look.

Flexibility

Examining a fabric's flexibility is another means of checking its ability to drape. Flexibility, as the term is used in this book, refers to the ability of a material to fold softly into a swag. Fabric with a good flexibility will swag in smooth curves. Fabric with poor flexibility will tend to crack and be uneven when it is swagged (Figure 356). This quality of fabric was checked when the cowl neckline was drafted (page 144). Good flexibility is also important when a design calls for the material to end in gathers such as in the cuff of a sleeve.

The flexibility of a fabric may be determined by holding the material on the true bias at two points about eighteen inches apart. Move the hands together and notice whether the material drops into graceful curves or whether it tends to buckle and crack.

Some materials will drape fairly well but will not have good flexibility. Other materials will both drape well and have good flexibility. Still others will drape poorly and have good flexibility.

Elasticity

Elasticity is the ability of a fabric to stretch. It is not an important quality for most woven goods but it will become very important for moderate stretch knits.

To check the elasticity of a fabric, hold it at two points approximately eighteen inches apart and stretch it. This check should be run with the horizontal threads, the vertical threads, and across the bias of the fabric.

Most woven fabrics will not stretch at all on the vertical threads. These are the threads that pull the fabric through the loom. They may stretch slightly on the horizontal filling threads. They will stretch considerably on the bias. The stretch in knits varies according to the specific way they are constructed.

Body and Weight

The body of a fabric is its mass or substance. The weight of a fabric is its actual weight in ounces per square yard. Normally the two are related, but some fabrics have more body than their weight would indicate. A thick pellon, for instance, does not weigh that much more than a thin pellon.

What determines how much body will be needed in a fabric is the type of garment it is to be used for. Shirts and blouses, for instance, should be lightweight; too much body would be inappropriate for such garments. Pants and skirts, on the other hand, must have more body in order to hang and fit properly. Heavy outer garments, such as coats, should have the most body.

KNITS

PATTERNS FOR KNITS

FRONT

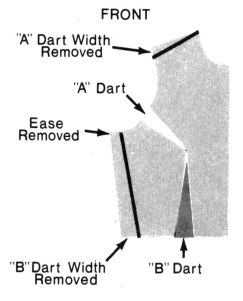

"A" Dart Width Removed

"A" Dart

Ease Removed

"B" Dart Width Removed

"B" Dart

BACK

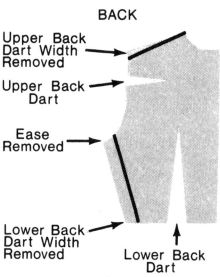

Upper Back Dart Width Removed

Upper Back Dart

Ease Removed

Lower Back Dart Width Removed

Lower Back Dart

Figure 357

This book has concentrated on developing patterns for woven fabrics. Woven fabrics are flat and they must be shaped to the contours of the body. Moderate stretch knits, on the other hand, are elastic. The fabric has the ability to shape itself to the contours of the body. Therefore, the patterns must be designed differently.

The patterns for moderate stretch knits will be different from patterns for woven fabrics in two ways. First, they will not require as much ease as the patterns seen thus far. Second, they may be created without darts.

The following procedure may be used to determine how much ease a knit will require.

Step 1. Lay out the fabric in the manner in which it is going to be cut. Knits usually stretch more along the width of the fabric than they do along the length. The direction with the most elasticity should be used around the body.

Step 2. On the fabric mark the dimension of the part of the body that is to be covered. For example, to draft a fitted top, mark off half the Front Bust measurement on the fabric.

Step 3. Stretch the fabric to see if it may be comfortably expanded to the size of the body plus the ease that would be allowed for a woven fabric. If it will, the stretch of the fabric may be used to replace the ease in the pattern.

Normally with a moderate stretch knit, the patterns should have about one inch of ease around the entire body. If the patterns are made the size of the body or even smaller than the body, the fabric will be kept in a constant state of tension.

Darts may be removed from patterns for knits because the stretch of the fabric will shape it to the contours of the body.

The shape for the Below the Bust contour, the lower back contour, and the Waist to Hip contour may be removed from the Side Seams. The

The Above the Bust contour and the Upper Back Dart for rounded backs may be removed by increasing the slope of the Shoulder Seams. Transfer these two darts to the appropriate Armhole Curve first. Then remove the width of these darts from the Armhole Curve by lowering the Shoulder Seam (Figure 357).

THE DRESS FORM

The basic patterns show the exact shape of the body they were fitted to. Therefore, these patterns may be cut out of a heavy cardboard and put together to create a duplicate of that figure. This cardboard shape may be used as a dress form.

The first step will be to remove the ease from the basic patterns so that the exact size of the body is established. The patterns for men may then be transferred to the cardboard and made into a body form.

For women an additional step is advisable. The basic patterns do not follow all of the contours of the bust exactly (see pages 163 to 165). Therefore, the dress form should be made to the size of the rib cage. The shape of the bust may then be duplicated by placing a stuffed bra on the form. Figure 358 shows the shape of the form without the bra and with the bra.

THE WOMAN'S DRESS FORM

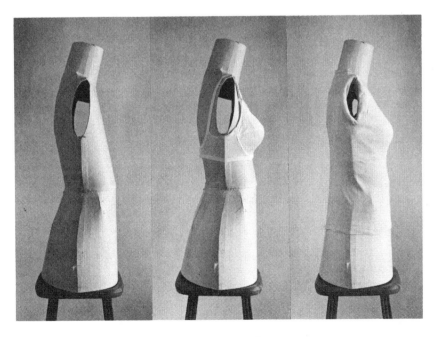

Figure 358

REMOVE THE EASE

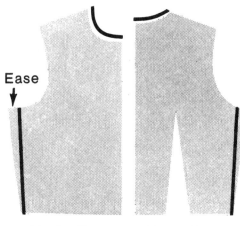

Ease

Man's Front   Man's Back

Figure 359

NECESSARY MATERIALS

Two sheets of 28" by 44" artists' matboard. This is non-corrugated cardboard that is about a sixteenth of an inch thick. It is thin enough to be shaped and heavy enough to keep its shape.

Tape Measure
Yardstick
Lightweight Wire Coathanger
Sharp Knife for cutting the matboard
Table Knife
Wide Masking Tape ($1\frac{1}{2}$" or more)
White Household Glue

REMOVING THE EASE

Step 1. Lay out the basic patterns and measure the distance from Center Front to the Side Seam to Center Back for the Bust (or Chest for men), the Waist, and the Hips. Record these measurements.

Step 2. From the Measurement Chart find the measurements for the Full Bust (#6) or the Chest (#4), the Waist (#11), and the Hips (#15). Divide these measurements in half and record the results.

Step 3. Subtract the results of the Measurement Chart from the measurements of the basic patterns. The difference between these two sets of measurements will show how much ease has been added to the basic patterns.

Step 4. On the basic patterns remove half the ease from the front pattern and half the ease from the back pattern. Figure 359 shows the altered basic patterns for a man.

Step 5. Make sure that the waist dimension of the bodice is the same as the waist dimension of the lower patterns.

Step 6. Measure the distance around the neck curve from Center Back to the Shoulder Seam to Center Front. Compare this length to half the Neck measurement (#1). If necessary, adjust the neck curve to make these measurements agree.

_____ Bust or Chest	minus _____ $\frac{1}{2}$ Bust (#6) or $\frac{1}{2}$ Chest (#4)	equals _____
_____ Waist	minus _____ $\frac{1}{2}$ Waist (#11)	equals _____
_____ Hips	minus _____ $\frac{1}{2}$ Hips (#15)	equals _____

MEASURING THE BACK

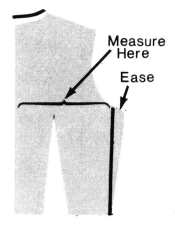

Figure 360

REMOVING THE BUST

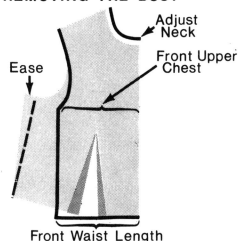

Figure 361

THE NECK PATTERN

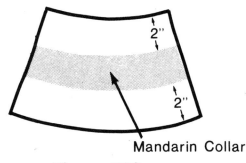

Figure 362

REMOVING THE BUST DIMENSION

Step 1. On the basic pattern measure the distance from the Center Back to the Side Seam at the bust height (Figure 360).

Step 2. Subtract this length from half the Upper Chest measurement (#5). The result is the Front Upper Chest Width.

Upper Chest Width

	minus		equals	
½ Upper Chest (#5)		Back Pattern Width		Front Width

Step 3. On the front basic pattern mark off the Front Upper Chest Width (Figure 361).

Step 4. Extend the Waist line out at right angles to the Center Front line.

Step 5. Measure the length of the Waist line on the basic pattern from the Center Front to the Side Seam excluding the length of the Dart Width. Mark this length on the new Waist line that is at right angles to Center Front. This establishes the Side Waist mark.

Step 6. Connect the Front Upper Chest Width mark to the new Side Waist mark. This is the Side Seam of the dress form.

Step 7. Measure the length of the back Side Seam and make the front Side Seam the same length. This will require dropping the Armhole Curve.

THE NECK PATTERN

Step 1. Take the Mandarin Collar pattern from pages 134 to 136. Extend the top up two inches and the bottom down two inches. Curve these two lines (Figure 362). This will be the neck pattern for the dress form.

PREPARE THE MAT BOARD

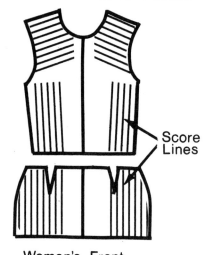

Score Lines

Woman's Front

Figure 363

REINFORCE SEAMS

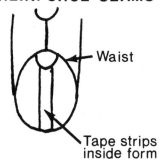

Waist

Tape strips inside form

Figure 364

ASSEMBLING THE FORM

Step 1. Transfer the pattern shapes to the mat board. Draw in the Center Front and Center Back line but do not cut these lines. Make the front one piece and the back one piece. There should only be a seam at the shoulder and the side of the form (Figure 363).

Step 2. Cut the mat board out along the seam and dart lines. Do not include any seam allowance.

Step 3. On the back side of the mat board, score indentations with the dull edge of a table knife. Figure 363 illustrates the direction these lines should take. This step breaks down the mat board slightly which will make it easier to bend smoothly.

Step 4. Bend the mat board to the shape of the body and tape the darts, the side seams, and the shoulder seams together with masking tape.

Step 5. Double check the dimensions around the dress form at the Chest, Waist, and Hips. Cut down the Side Seams if necessary.

Step 6. Cut one inch strips of mat board that are the lengths of the various seams.

Step 7. On the inside of the dress form place glue along the seam lines. Place the one inch strips over these seams and tape them in place (Figure 363). This step helps to take the edge off the seams of the dress form.

Step 8. Shape the neck pattern and tape it closed. Push it through the neck open from the inside of the form. The neck will help to shape the form.

Step 9. Adjust the pitch of the neck forwards or backwards to conform with the angle of the neck of the person the form is for. Tape the neck in place.

THE WAIST SHAPE

The next step is to determine the shape of the Waist. This will be a cross-sectional view of the body. This Waist Circle will hold the shape of the dress form. It may be cut out of wood and nailed in place or it may be cut out of mat board and taped in place.

Step 1. On a piece of paper draw two lines at right angles to each other (Figure 365).

Step 2. Measure the distance straight across the body from one side of the waist to the other. Mark this length on one of the lines.

THE WAIST CIRCLE

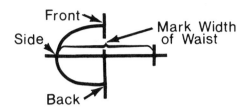

Figure 365

MEASURING THE BODY

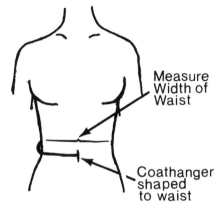

Measure Width of Waist

Coathanger shaped to waist

Figure 366

ADDING THE WAIST CIRCLE

Strips inside waist

Tape Waist Circle in place

Figure 367

DRESS FORM STAND

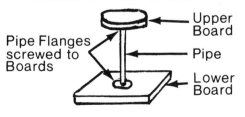

Pipe Flanges screwed to Boards

Upper Board

Pipe

Lower Board

Figure 368

Step 3. Measure the distance on the body from the front of the waist to the back of the waist and mark this on the other line.

Step 4. Take a lightweight wire coathanger and shape it around the waist from the Center Front to the Center Back (Figure 366). Place the coathanger on the paper and draw in this shape.

Step 5. Measure the distance around the circumference of this circle. Adjust the circle in or out until this measurement is slightly less than half the Waist measurement (#11).

Step 6. Fold the paper in half to shape the other side.

This shape may now be transferred either to wood or the mat board. A mat board waist will require the following steps.

Step 7. Tape one inch strips of mat board an eighth of an inch in from the inside edge of the waist on the form (Figure 367).

Step 8. Place the mat board Waist Circle on the rim and tape it in place.

Step 9. Tape the Waist to Hip part of the form to the upper part of the dress form.

This dress form may not have all of the curves of the body exactly the same as the curves of your body but the dimensions will be correct for fitting purposes. To check the fit, place your fitted muslin on the dress form. It should fit the form just as well as it fits you.

DRESS FORM STANDS

Various types of stands may be worked out for this dress form.

A very sturdy stand may be made from two pieces of wood, two pipe flanges (available at any hardware store), a length of pipe, and eight wood screws.

The bottom piece of wood should be wider than the dress form for maximum support. The upper piece of wood should be cut as close to the size of the Waist Circle as possible. This piece of wood may be glued directly into the form after the pipe flange has been mounted on it. The pipe may be cut to the right length to make the form the same height as the person it has been made for.

A less permanent base is a tall bar stool. The dress form may be taped onto this stool to keep it from shifting around.

ALTERING COMMERCIAL PATTERNS

Commercial patterns will provide a good reference source for creating original patterns. They will show the lines for the latest fashions. They will give design details for involved tailored patterns. And they may be used as guidelines to determine the amounts of ease and/or fullness to give various designs. Therefore, it is important to be able to evaluate commercial patterns and adjust them for fit.

Each commercial pattern company has developed sets of standard fitted patterns. These patterns are designed to fit a standardized body the same way the fitted patterns in this book are designed to fit you. The standardized body shape they use is designed to resemble as many people as possible. All of a companies designs will be adjusted to fit this standard shape.

Several of the pattern companies sell copies of their basic fitted patterns which they refer to as "Personal Fitting Patterns." By comparing their Personal Fitting Patterns to your basic fitted patterns, you will be able to tell the differences between your shape and the standard figure. By comparing their Personal Fitting Patterns to their designed patterns, you will be able to tell what alterations they have made to the basic patterns to achieve a given design.

COMPARING BASIC PATTERNS

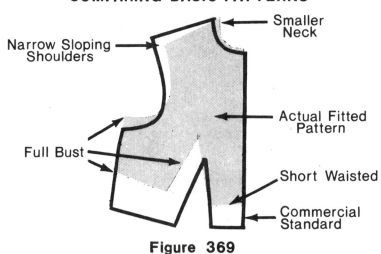

Figure 369

184

ANALYZING DESIGNS

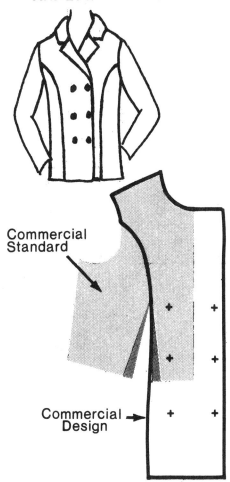

Commercial Standard

Commercial Design

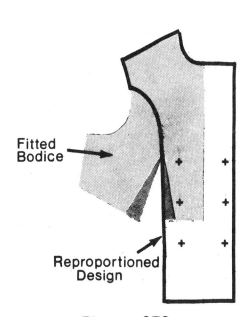

Fitted Bodice

Reproportioned Design

Figure 370

COMPARING BASIC PATTERNS

Purchase the Personal Fitting Pattern in the size you normally buy from the company you prefer to patronize.

Spread out the Personal Fitting Patterns and lay a sheet of tracing paper over them. Trace around the front bodice pattern pivoting out the side dart. The Personal Fitting Pattern should now have a single dart to the waist (Figure 369).

Lay the traced Personal Fitting Pattern on top of your basic fitted pattern. Match the Shoulder Seam and Center Front. Trace your basic fitted pattern with a red pen. The differences between the commercial Personal Fitting Pattern and your basic fitted pattern show exactly how much and where you must change the patterns of all the designs you purchase from this particular company.

If your shoulders slope more than the Personal Fitting Patterns, you will have to change the shoulder slope on all designs. Differences in the Armhole Curve and Neck Curves will also have to be adjusted in all designs.

Adjusting the bust dart may present certain problems. Basically, commercial patterns only have two sizes for the "A" Dart Width. Butterick, for instance, sizes all Misses, Miss Petit, Junior, and Junior Petit patterns for the same "A" Dart Width. Their Dart Width corresponds to the two inch line on the chart on page 53. This is basically a "B" cup bra. The Women's patterns are styled to correspond to the three inch line on the chart.

For a smaller bust the dart size will have to be decreased, the armhole lowered, and the Side Seam adjusted. For a larger bust size the dart size will have to be increased, the armhole raised, and the Side Seam adjusted.

COMPARING THE BASIC PATTERNS TO A DESIGN

Some figures will vary considerably from the standard shapes. This may require too many changes to be practical. In this case, it is better to compare the commercial companies designed pattern to their Personal Fitting Pattern. Note the changes the design has made to the Personal Fitting Pattern and make the same changes to your basic fitted pattern.

INDEX

FRACTIONAL CHART

The fractional scales on the opposite page provide a way of dividing measurements without having to figure the answers out in your head.

To use this chart locate the correct scale, either the half scale or the quarter scale. Then find the number to be divided in the "A" column. The answer will be found in the "B" column. For example, to find half of six look at the first scale. Opposite 6 in the "A" column is 3 in the "B" column. Half of six is three.

The chart is also divided into fractions of an inch. These fractions are indicated at the top of each scale. For instance, one half of $37\frac{1}{2}$ is $18\frac{3}{4}$.

The "B" columns are in actual inches. The answers found in this column may be compared directly to a yardstick or tape measure.

FRACTIONAL CHART

HALF SCALE | QUARTER SCALE

HALF SCALE

Column 1: 0 A B 0 | 1/4 | 1/2 — 1/4 | 3/4 | 1 — 1/2 | 1/4 | 1/2 — 3/4 | 3/4 | 2 — 1 | 3 | 4 — 2 | 5 | 6 — 3 | 7 | 8 — 4 | 9 | 10 — 5 | 11 | 12 — 6 | 13 | 14 — 7 | 15 | 16 — 8 | 17 | 18 — 9

Column 2: 18 A B 9 | 1/4 | 1/2 — 1/4 | 3/4 | 19 — 1/2 | 1/4 | 1/2 — 3/4 | 3/4 | 20 — 10 | 21 | 22 — 11 | 23 | 24 — 12 | 25 | 26 — 13 | 27 | 28 — 14 | 29 | 30 — 15 | 31 | 32 — 16 | 33 | 34 — 17 | 35 | 36 — 18

Column 3: 36 A B 18 | 1/4 | 1/2 — 1/4 | 3/4 | 37 — 1/2 | 1/4 | 1/2 — 3/4 | 3/4 | 38 — 19 | 39 | 40 — 20 | 41 | 42 — 21 | 43 | 44 — 22 | 45 | 46 — 23 | 47 | 48 — 24 | 49 | 50 — 25 | 51 | 52 — 26 | 53 | 54 — 27

QUARTER SCALE

Column 4: 0 A B 0 | 1/2 | 1 — 1/4 | 1/2 | 2 — 1/2 | 1/2 | 3 — 3/4 | 1/2 | 4 — 1 | 5 | 6 | 7 | 8 — 2 | 9 | 10 | 11 | 12 — 3 | 13 | 14 | 15 | 16 — 4 | 17 | 18 | 19 | 20 — 5 | 21 | 22 | 23 | 24 — 6 | 25 | 26 | 27 | 28 — 7 | 29 | 30 | 31 | 32 — 8 | 33 | 34 | 35 | 36 — 9

Column 5: 36 A B 9 | 1/2 | 37 — 1/4 | 1/2 | 38 — 1/2 | 1/2 | 39 — 3/4 | 1/2 | 40 — 10 | 41 | 42 | 43 | 44 — 11 | 45 | 46 | 47 | 48 — 12 | 49 | 50 | 51 | 52 — 13 | 53 | 54 | 55 | 56 — 14 | 57 | 58 | 59 | 60 — 15 | 61 | 62 | 63 | 64 — 16 | 65 | 66 | 67 | 68 — 17 | 69 | 70

189

BODY SILHOUETTES

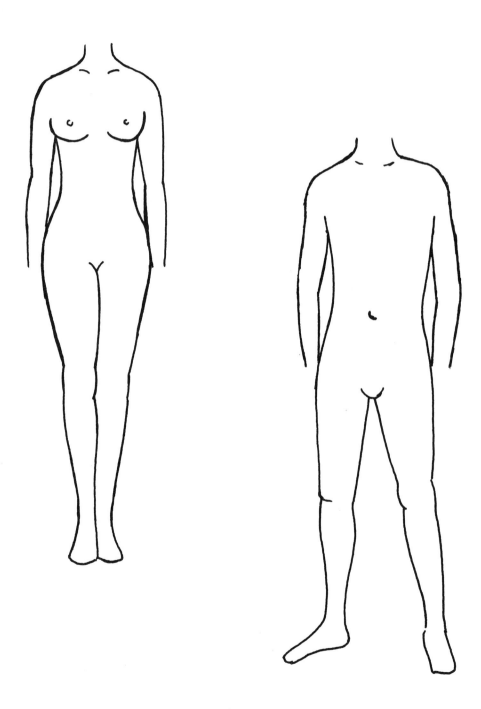